OF EAST AFRICA

CHRIS & TILDE STUART

Struik Nature
(an imprint of Random House Struik (Pty) Ltd)
Wembley Square 2, First Floor, Solan Road, Gardens, Cape Town, 8001
PO Box 1144, Cape Town, 8000 South Africa

Company Reg. No. 1966/003153/07

Visit **www.randomstruik.co.za** and join the Struik Nature Club
for updates, news, events, and special offers.

First published 2009

5 7 9 10 8 6

Publisher: Pippa Parker
Managing editor: Helen de Villiers
Project manager: Emily Bowles
Editor: Cynthia Kemp
Design director: Janice Evans
Designer: Martin Endemann
Proofreader: Tessa Kennedy

Reproduction by Hirt & Carter Cape (Pty) Ltd
Printed and bound by Times Offset (M) Sdn Bhd, Malaysia

ISBN 978 1 77007 706 5

Front cover: Lion
Back cover, top to bottom: Zanzibar red colobus,
porcupine quills, Sharpe's grysbok, leopard spots, caracal
Title page: Uganda kob; Opposite: Cheetah

Acknowledgements

We would like to thank those who helped fill our photographic blanks, as listed under
photographic credits. Jonathan Kingdon is thanked for helping us unravel the complexities
of certain Swahili mammal names. Special thanks go to Pippa Parker (publishing manager) for
suggesting this title, to Cynthia Kemp for a fine editing job, and to the rest of the Struik team
Helen de Villiers, Emily Bowles, Janice Evans and Martin Endemann, for pulling it all together.

CONTENTS

INTRODUCTION

The name 'East Africa' conjures up vistas of grassland scattered with umbrella thorn trees, and home to vast herds of hoofed mammals. Yet the region is comprised not only of this, but of many different habitats, from high mountains to rain forests, great lakes and rivers to coastline, all providing suitable living space for more than 360 species of terrestrial mammal. The mammal species range in size from elephants that may weigh several thousand kilograms, to bats, shrews and mice that tip the scales at little more than a few grams.

AREA COVERED BY THIS GUIDE

Politically, East Africa consists of **Kenya**, **Uganda**, **Tanzania**, **Burundi** and **Rwanda**. However, wildlife in the last-mentioned two countries has largely been eradicated. To the east lies the Indian Ocean and to the west are the four great lakes – Edward, Victoria, Tanganyika and Malawi. Here are the legendary Ruwenzoris, or Mountains of the Moon, and the mighty peaks of Kilimanjaro, Kenya and Elgon. A chain of soda lakes runs like an uneven necklace down the floor of the Great Rift Valley. Where the mighty Nile River rises there are active, dormant and long-dead volcanoes. It is a region not only of great topographical diversity but also of numerous vegetation types.

The vegetation map (page 6) has been greatly simplified but does indicate seven of the most important vegetation types that you will encounter during your East African travels. Outside the conservation areas much of the landscape has been greatly modified by the actions of growing human populations. Large tracts of natural bushland have been cleared for agriculture, both subsistence and commercial, and trees have been turned into charcoal. Human settlements have increased and existing ones have expanded. Poaching has resulted in decreasing mammal diversity and populations. Nevertheless, those interested in wildlife, and specifically in mammals, have much to look forward to in the region.

We have included most of the larger and more conspicuous mammal species. In addition, a few of the more unusual species such as the pangolin, aardvark and porcupine have been included, as well as representatives from the different families and genera of bats, shrews, elephant shrews (sengis) and smaller rodents.

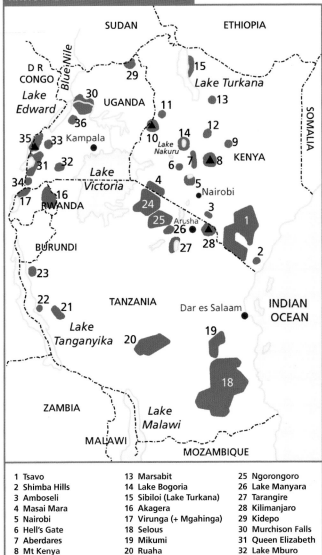

NATIONAL PARKS & GAME RESERVES

1 Tsavo	13 Marsabit	25 Ngorongoro
2 Shimba Hills	14 Lake Bogoria	26 Lake Manyara
3 Amboseli	15 Sibiloi (Lake Turkana)	27 Tarangire
4 Masai Mara	16 Akagera	28 Kilimanjaro
5 Nairobi	17 Virunga (+ Mgahinga)	29 Kidepo
6 Hell's Gate	18 Selous	30 Murchison Falls
7 Aberdares	19 Mikumi	31 Queen Elizabeth
8 Mt Kenya	20 Ruaha	32 Lake Mburo
9 Meru	21 Katavi	33 Kibale
10 Mt Elgon	22 Mahale	34 Bwindi
11 Saiwa Swamp	23 Gombe	35 Ruwenzori
12 Samburu complex	24 Serengeti	36 Budongo

VEGETATION MAP

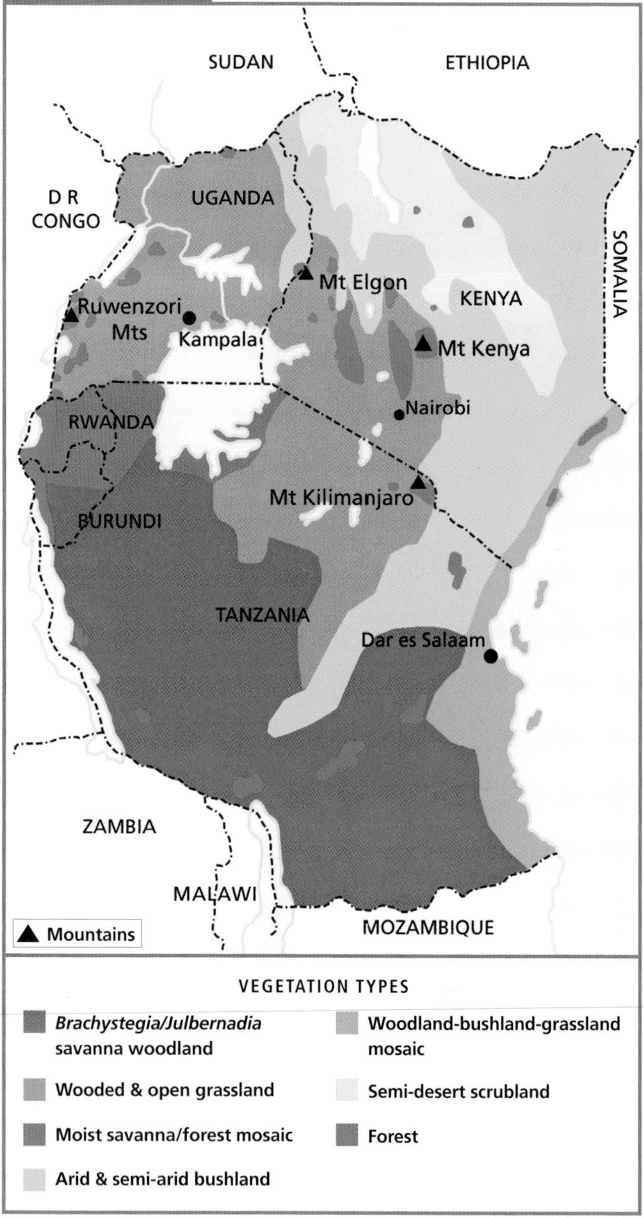
SUDAN
ETHIOPIA
UGANDA
D R
CONGO
SOMALIA
Mt Elgon
KENYA
Ruwenzori
Mts
Kampala
Mt Kenya
Nairobi
RWANDA
Mt Kilimanjaro
BURUNDI
TANZANIA
Dar es Salaam
ZAMBIA
MALAWI
MOZAMBIQUE
Mountains
VEGETATION TYPES
Brachystegia/Julbernadia savanna woodland
Woodland-bushland-grassland mosaic
Wooded & open grassland
Semi-desert scrubland
Moist savanna/forest mosaic
Forest
Arid & semi-arid bushland

Brachystegia/Julbernadia savanna woodland

Woodland-bushland-grassland mosaic

Wooded & open grassland

Semi-desert scrubland

Moist savanna/forest mosaic

Forest

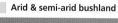

Arid & semi-arid bushland

HOW TO USE THIS GUIDE

Information is compiled with a view to easy identification of the larger and more conspicuous mammals of East Africa, as well as a few of the less frequently seen, yet distinctive, species.

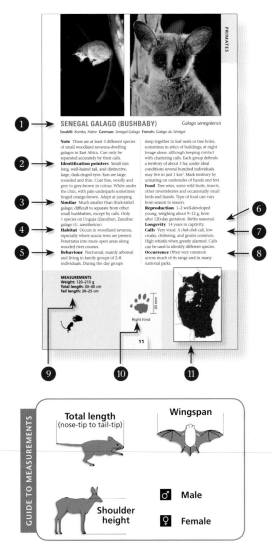

PRIMATES

SENEGAL GALAGO (BUSHBABY)　　*Galago senegalensis*

Swahili: *Komba, Ndere* **German:** *Senegal-Galago* **French:** *Galago du Sénégal*

Note There are at least 3 different species of small woodland savanna-dwelling galagos in East Africa. Can only be separated accurately by their calls.

Identification pointers Small size; long, well-haired tail, and distinctive, large, dark-ringed eyes. Ears are large, rounded and thin. Coat fine, woolly and grey to grey-brown in colour. White under the chin, with pale underparts sometimes tinged orange-brown. Adept at jumping.

Similar Much smaller than thick-tailed galago; difficult to separate from other small bushbabies, except by calls. Only 1 species on Unguja (Zanzibar), Zanzibar galago (*G. zanzibaricus*).

Habitat Occurs in woodland savanna, especially where acacia trees are present. Penetrates into more open areas along wooded river courses.

Behaviour Nocturnal, mainly arboreal and living in family groups of 2–8 individuals. During the day groups sleep together in leaf nests or tree holes, sometimes in attics of buildings; at night forage alone, although keeping contact with chattering calls. Each group defends a territory of about 3 ha; under ideal conditions several hundred individuals may live in just 1 km². Mark territory by urinating on undersides of hands and feet.

Food Tree resin, some wild fruits, insects, other invertebrates and occasionally small birds and lizards. Type of food can vary from season to season.

Reproduction 1–2 well-developed young, weighing about 9–12 g, born after 120-day gestation. Births seasonal.

Longevity 14 years in captivity.

Calls Very vocal. A *chek-chek* call, low croaks, chittering, and grunts common. High whistle when greatly alarmed. Calls can be used to identify different species.

Occurrence Often very common across much of its range and in many national parks.

MEASUREMENTS
Weight: 120–210 g
Total length: 30–40 cm
Tail length: 20–25 cm

Right hind

30 mm

11

GUIDE TO MEASUREMENTS

Total length
(nose-tip to tail-tip)

Wingspan

Shoulder height

♂ Male

♀ Female

❶ **Name:** The common English name is given, as well as those in Swahili, German and French. Swahili names may vary; the most frequently used are listed. For species occurring outside the main language area, Swahili names may not exist.

❷ **Identification pointers:** Presented without using scientific jargon.

❸ **Similar:** Names of similar species, or those in the East African region with which a species is commonly confused.

❹ **Habitat:** This is often an important aid to identifying a mammal, especially in conjunction with the distribution map.

❺ **Behaviour, Food and Reproduction:** These are added for interest, but also aid identification. If a species is known to be solitary and you think you have seen it in a large herd, read through the text describing behaviour in order to establish an alternative identity.

❻ **Longevity:** Information on roughly how long the species is known to live.

❼ **Calls:** The most frequently heard calls are given.

❽ **Occurrence:** This gives the major reserves in which a species occurs, its conservation status and known numbers.

❾ **Measurements:** Those of male and female are given separately where the two differ significantly. Also includes silhouette drawings of the species, with a human figure for comparison of scale. For so-called 'trophy' species, we have given the Rowland Ward records for East Africa. Larger specimens may be known beyond the region.

❿ **Tracks:** Drawings of typical tracks (where available) add interest and serve also as tools for species identification.

⓫ **Distribution map:** Illustrates range across which the species has been recorded.

NOTE

SUCCESSFUL MAMMAL WATCHING

To best observe the mammals covered in this guide you will require a pair of binoculars. Once you have spotted a mammal, try to establish the group to which it belongs (is it a cat or a dog or an antelope?). If possible, estimate height at shoulder level, or guess total length in relation to the tail (is the tail the same length as the head and body, or is it much shorter?). Are there any outstanding features, such as a bushy tail, spots, stripes or particularly long ears? In the case of an antelope be sure to note the shape of the horns, and whether they are smooth, strongly ridged or only partly ringed. Remember that young animals may in some cases resemble adults of another species, particularly when seen in stages of early horn development. Make a note of any particular behavioural traits or peculiarities. Was the animal in a group or solitary? Was it in a tree? Did it run down a burrow?

Look out for spoor, or tracks, most easily seen in mud or sand. Fresh tracks may even give insight into animal activities, without your even observing them. Likewise, an animal's droppings provide a useful indicator of its presence – see the dung identification section appearing after the species accounts.

POTTO

Perodicticus potto

Swahili: – **German:** *Potto* **French:** *Potto*

Identification pointers Small but stockily built with very short tail, short-snouted face, large eyes and small, rounded ears. Hands and feet are well developed. Coat is thick and woolly and varies in colour from reddish-brown to greyish-brown, with paler underparts. Snout usually lighter than rest of face.

Similar Shares habitat with a number of galago species, but galagos have long tails and much larger ears.

Habitat Occurs in primary and secondary forest, preferring areas with dense and tangled undergrowth.

Behaviour Solitary, nocturnal, and arboreal and only rarely moves on the ground. During the day they sleep on slender branches among dense vegetation cover. Home ranges cover from 7–12 ha in some areas. Male is territorial and marks territory with urine on upper surfaces of larger branches. The potto is said to give off a strong curry-like odour. When foraging, moves slowly and deliberately along branches.

Food Wide range of wild fruits, tree resin, insects and other invertebrates. Also hunts small vertebrates such as rodents, bats, birds and probably chameleons.

Reproduction In East Africa young are born mainly in November to February but also in other months. Young (usually single, rarely twins), weighing 35–50 g, are dropped after about a 190-day gestation.

Longevity Up to 11 years in captivity; 1 individual reached 26 years.

Calls May growl, but mostly quiet. Mother and young give a high-pitched *tisc* contact call.

Occurrence Occurs in Mgahinga, Bwindi, Queen Elizabeth, Kibale, Budongo, Mt Elgon (Uganda); Mt Elgon, Kakamega (Kenya). May be threatened in places by loss of habitat, but common in some forests.

MEASUREMENTS
Weight: 600 g–1.6 kg
Total length: 30–50 cm
Tail length: 5–8 cm

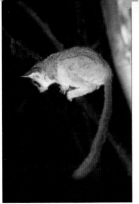

SENEGAL GALAGO (BUSHBABY)

Galago senegalensis

Swahili: *Komba, Ndere* **German:** *Senegal-Galago* **French:** *Galago du Sénégal*

Note There are at least 3 different species of small woodland savanna-dwelling galagos in East Africa. Can only be separated accurately by their calls.

Identification pointers Small size; long, well-haired tail, and distinctive, large, dark-ringed eyes. Ears are large, rounded and thin. Coat fine, woolly and grey to grey-brown in colour. White under the chin, with pale underparts sometimes tinged orange-brown. Adept at jumping.

Similar Much smaller than thick-tailed galago; difficult to separate from other small bushbabies, except by calls. Only one species on Unguja (Zanzibar), Zanzibar galago (*G. zanzibaricus*).

Habitat Occurs in woodland savanna, especially where acacia trees are present. Penetrates into more open areas along wooded river courses.

Behaviour Nocturnal, mainly arboreal and living in family groups of 2–8 individuals. During the day groups sleep together in leaf nests or tree holes, sometimes in attics of buildings; at night forage alone, although keeping contact with chattering calls. Each group defends a territory of about 3 ha; under ideal conditions several hundred individuals may live in just 1 km². Mark territory by urinating on undersides of hands and feet.

Food Tree resin, some wild fruits, insects, other invertebrates and occasionally small birds and lizards. Type of food can vary from season to season.

Reproduction 1–2 well-developed young, weighing about 9–12 g, born after 120-day gestation. Births seasonal.

Longevity 14 years in captivity.

Calls Very vocal. A *chek-chek* call, low croaks, chittering, and grunts common. High whistle when greatly alarmed. Calls can be used to identify different species.

Occurrence Often very common across much of its range and in many national parks.

MEASUREMENTS
Weight: 120–210 g
Total length: 30–40 cm
Tail length: 20–25 cm

Right front

30 mm

DWARF GALAGO

Galago demidoff

Swahili: *Komba kidogo* **German:** *Zwerggalago* **French:** *Galago de Demidoff*

Identification pointers Smallest bushbaby in region, with narrow head and slightly upturned muzzle. Ears rather smaller than other galagos. Fur colour variable from greyish-brown, dark grey to bright ginger-brown. Dark eye-rings and white facial blaze common. Tail not bushy.

Similar Smaller than Senegal galago, also separated by habitat; in western Uganda other galago species much larger and often more numerous.

Habitat Lowland and montane forest up to about 2 000 m above sea level, bamboo thicket, swamp and riverine forest. Strong preference for vegetation ranging from near ground level to about 10 m.

Behaviour Social animals living in groups of up to 12 individuals but foraging alone and maintaining contact with calls. After foraging, individuals of group reunite at dawn. During the day they rest in crude leaf nests with most activity taking place at night. Mainly arboreal. Several females may sleep together in groups of 2–10. As with other bushbabies, they mark their territory with urine sprayed onto undersides of hands and feet.

Food Mainly insects, especially caterpillars, beetles and crickets, but will also eat tree resin and wild fruits.

Reproduction 1–2 young, after a gestation of about 110 days. Well developed at birth and able to move around by second day. Female grasps young in her mouth to move them.

Longevity 10 years in captivity.

Calls Frequently repeated, shrill, rasping *chink* for a few seconds; *burr*-chittering noises and a harsh alarm call.

Occurrence Very common in some Ugandan forests: Mgahinga; Bwindi; Queen Elizabeth; Kibale; Budongo.

MEASUREMENTS
Weight: 95–120 g
Total length: 27.5–37 cm
Tail length: 15–21.5 cm

Right front

20 mm

■ Dwarf galago

THICK-TAILED (GREATER) GALAGO
Otolemur crassicaudatus

Swahili: *Komba* **German:** *Riesengalago* **French:** *Galago à queue épaisse*

Identification pointers Largest of the galagos, with large ears and eyes, dense and soft fur varying in colour from grey to grey-brown to almost black. Tail is long-haired and bushy. On ground rather cat-like, rump higher than shoulders and tail often held erect. A second species, Garnett's thick-tailed galago, very similar and ranges overlap in East Africa.

Similar Other galagos in East Africa very much smaller.

Habitat Preference for dense, dry woodland and riverine forest; montane forests up to 3 500 m above sea level. Frequently in orchards, plantations and large, wooded gardens.

Behaviour Nocturnal, spending daylight hours in dense vegetation or self-constructed leaf nests. Although they live in groups of 2–6 individuals, they forage alone and males sleep apart from females and offspring. Each group lives in a fixed and scent-demarcated home range, and, in suitable habitat, they may occur in large numbers (125 individuals in 1 km²). Spend more time foraging on ground than other galagos.

Food Mainly wild fruits and tree resin (especially acacia), but also insects, other invertebrates; occasionally reptiles and birds.

Reproduction Usually 2 young (rarely triplets), each weighing 50–70 g, born after about 130-day gestation. Young are dropped just before start of rainy season – mainly August to November.

Longevity Up to 14 years in captivity.

Calls One of African woodland savanna's most distinctive nocturnal calls – a loud croaking scream, frequently repeated, especially after dusk and before dawn. Has been likened to a human baby in distress.

Occurrence Common across suitable habitat in East Africa and in most national parks.

MEASUREMENTS
Weight: 1–1.5 kg
Total length: 70–80 cm
Tail length: 35–45 cm

Right
back

50 mm

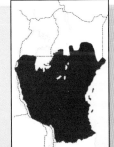

1 **2**

SAVANNA BABOON

Papio cynocephalus (hamadryas)

Swahili: *Nyani* **German:** *Steppenpavian* **French:** *Babouin*

Identification pointers Relatively slender and long-limbed build, with males larger than females. When standing or walking, shoulders are higher than rump, and characteristic 'broken' (inverted u-shape) tail is diagnostic. Elongated and dog-like muzzle is especially well developed in males. Two races occur: **1** yellow baboon (*P. cynocephalus*) with yellowish-brown coat, and **2** olive baboon that is overall olive-greenish. Males of olive race have a very well-developed cape on shoulders.

Similar No other similar primate in region; chimpanzee black, with no tail.

Habitat Usually associated with wooded savanna but also found in mountainous and hilly country. Access to drinking water essential, as well as to roosting cliffs or tall trees.

Behaviour Highly social, living in troops of 15–100 individuals. Adult males (>5 years) dominant over females and there is a strict pecking order. Dominant male determines when troop will move or rest and usually has sole mating rights with receptive females.

Food True omnivores, feeding on a wide range of plant and animal food, including young antelope, hares and mice that are actively hunted (usually by adult males). In agricultural areas can be a nuisance, raiding crops and killing livestock.

Reproduction Single, pink-faced young born after about 180-day gestation and for first few weeks of life it clings to chest hair of its mother when on the move. Births occur at any time of year.

Longevity At least 30 years (45 known) in captivity.

Calls Very vocal, far-carrying *bogum* bark; grunting, squealing, chattering and screaming.

Occurrence In many national parks. Common throughout range; hunted in some areas.

MEASUREMENTS
Weight: ♂ 25–45 kg;
♀ 12–28 kg
Shoulder height: 40–75 cm
Total length: ♂ 1.2–1.8 m;
♀ 1–1.2 m
Tail length: 50–85 cm

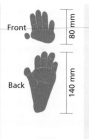

Front
80 mm

Back
140 mm

■ Olive baboon
■ Yellow baboon
■ Overlap

VERVET MONKEY

Cercopithecus pygerythrus

Swahili: *Tumbili, Ngedere* **German:** *Grünmeerkatze* **French:** *Grivet*

Identification pointers Typical monkey-like appearance with long tail, black face with white brow-band and coat grizzled-grey, sometimes with yellowish-olive infusion. Underparts paler to white, upper surfaces of hands and feet usually black, and scrotum of male powder blue.

Similar Should not be mistaken for any other monkey.

Habitat Savanna and riverine wood-land, often penetrating into arid areas and coastal scrub forest. In some parts occurs up to 4 000 m above sea level in montane forest and its fringes. Has greatest range of any African monkey.

Behaviour More terrestrial than any other long-tailed monkey (except much larger patas). Can live in troops of 20 or more individuals, but most groups tend to be smaller. Diurnal, sleeping at night in trees and, rarely, on cliffs. Much of their foraging is done on the ground.

In each troop clear social ranking is well established and maintained. Troops are multi-male and multi-female, with little conflict between troop individuals.

Food Wide range of fruits, flowers, leaves, seeds and resin, as well as insects and small vertebrates. Can become a nuisance in farming areas, raiding crops.

Reproduction Births may occur at any time of year, but there are definite peaks in the number of young born. Single young dropped after gestation of about 165 days. Newborns have pink faces.

Longevity 31 years in captivity.

Calls Quiet coughing and gargling contact noises; harsh chattering and repeated sharp barking when threatened, or when conflict occurs between troops.

Occurrence Common throughout its range, often in close proximity to human settlements and in many national parks and reserves.

MEASUREMENTS
Weight: ♂ 4–8 kg;
  ♀ 3.5–5 kg
Total length: ♂ 1–1.3 m;
  ♀ 95 cm–1.1 m
Tail length: ♂ 60–75 cm;
  ♀ 48–65 cm

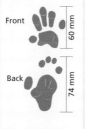

Front — 60 mm

Back — 74 mm

SYKES'S MONKEY

Cercopithecus albogularis

Swahili: *Nchima, Kima* **German:** *Weißkehlmeerkatze* **French:** *Cercopithèque à collier blanc*

Identification pointers At least 10 races recognised in East Africa. Typical monkey appearance. In most races hair relatively long and dark, especially on upper surfaces of hands and feet as well as limbs. Long facial whiskers. Some races have prominent white throat ruff (Mt Kenya), others overall very dark (Aberdares, Mt Elgon, Queen Elizabeth). One of the most frequently encountered forest monkeys, often heard not seen.

Similar In western Uganda see grey-cheeked mangabey.

Habitat Lowland and montane forest (to above 3 000 m), swamp forest and high-altitude bamboo thickets. On coast, in relatively low scrub forest, and on Unguja (Zanzibar) utilises mangrove woodland.

Behaviour Live in troops of up to 40 individuals; often fewer. Most troops controlled by single adult male. Only females defend troop territory, while principal male chases off other males. Spend much of their foraging time in trees but regularly on ground too. In East Africa commonly mix with other forest monkey species. Troop home range size dictated by conditions. In ideal conditions there may be up to 300 individuals to 1 km², but generally range covers a smaller area.

Food Very wide variety of plants, including leaves, fruits, seeds, flowers and resin. They eat some insects, and have been seen catching birds and small mammals, including bushbabies.

Reproduction Single young, about 400 g, after some 120–140 days.

Longevity 20 years, perhaps older.

Calls Range of calls, but most obvious is male's loud, far-carrying *jack* or *pyow* call.

Occurrence Most races still common and sometimes abundant, but a few endangered – such as the 'golden' race (*C. a. kandti*) in a limited area of the Virunga volcanoes.

MEASUREMENTS
Weight: ♂ 8–10 kg; ♀ 4–5 kg
Total length: ♂ 1.4 m; ♀ 1.2 m
Tail length: ♂ 80 cm; ♀ 70 cm

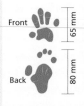

Front 65 mm

Back 80 mm

DE BRAZZA'S MONKEY

Cercopithecus neglectus

Swahili: *Kalasinga* **German:** *Brazza-Meerkatze* **French:** *Cercopithèque de Brazza*

Identification pointers Fairly stocky monkey with a long, somewhat thickened tail. Overall colour is greeny-grey but there is a distinctive white stripe running down outer surface of thigh and the tail is black. There is a bright orange-red brow stripe backed by a black band. Muzzle and longish beard are white.

Similar Only monkey in region with prominent white beard and thigh stripe.

Habitat Mainly swamp forest but also montane and lowland forest, including bamboo thickets. Occupies dry montane forest to at least 2 100 m above sea level.

Behaviour Feed on the ground as well as in trees, and live in troops of between 15 and 35 individuals. A single adult male leads the larger troops, and solitary males are quite frequently encountered. Unlike most monkeys, they are said to be good swimmers. They will flee from danger, but are also adept at freezing for

long periods, thus avoiding detection.

Food Mixed diet of plant parts, but fruits and seeds most important. Readily feed on insects and other invertebrates. They have been reported raiding crops, especially millet.

Reproduction Births apparently take place at any time, but seasonal peaks occur in some areas. A single young, weighing about 250 g, is dropped after a 182-day gestation.

Longevity Up to 22 years.

Calls Rather quiet monkeys, with grunting, chittering alarm croak uttered by male: *chi-chi-chi-aarh* ending with croaking barks. A booming hoot sometimes given.

Occurrence Numbers stable in Uganda, but considered endangered in Kenya. Kibale, Bwamba, Mt Elgon (Uganda); Mt Elgon, Kakamega (Kenya).

MEASUREMENTS
Weight: ♂ 5–8 kg; ♀ 4–5 kg
Total length: ♂ 1.1–1.4 m;
♀ 95 cm–1.1 m
Tail length: 53–85 cm

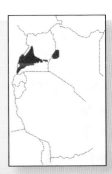

L'HOEST'S GUENON

Cercopithecus l'hoesti

Swahili: – **German:** *Vollbartmeerkatze* **French:** *Cercopithèque de l'Hoest*

Identification pointers A very dark coloured, long-tailed monkey with strongly contrasting white cheek and throat hair. Much of the coat is very dark brown to black, but the back is usually infused with reddish-brown in an oval-shaped saddle. Lips and nose black and remainder of face pale grey to pinkish-grey. Tail held strongly hooked over back when on the move.

Similar Should not be confused with other monkeys in limited range, but see local races of Sykes's monkey; compare tail posture.

Habitat Montane forest; also lowland rain forest and gallery forest, as well as well-wooded mountain slopes. Sometimes called 'mountain monkey'.

Behaviour Move about and feed in trees, undergrowth and quite often on the ground. Troop size ranges from 10–17 animals, occasionally more, and each with only 1 adult male. Within

their Ugandan range, troop home ranges cover about 7–10 km², which is unusually large for a forest monkey. They are commonly seen mixing with other monkey and guenon species in some locations. They are very alert monkeys and troop members frequently climb to vantage points, making them difficult to approach.

Food Wide range of plant foods, with fruits being of particular importance. Known to raid croplands, even hundreds of metres from forest.

Reproduction There is a birth-peak from December to February, but young have been recorded at other times. No other information in the wild.

Longevity Not known.

Calls Short alarm bark – *hack*; contact chirps.

Occurrence Present in a number of western Ugandan forests: Queen Elizabeth, Kibale, Ruwenzori, Bwindi.

MEASUREMENTS
Weight: ♂ 5–8 kg; ♀ 3–4 kg
Total length: 1.1–1.5 kg
Tail length: 48–80 cm

OWL-FACED GUENON

Cercopithecus hamlyni

Swahili: – **German:** *Eulenkopfaffe* **French:** *Cercopithèque à tête de hibou*

Identification pointers A medium-sized, long-tailed monkey with a large, rounded, owl-like face clearly marked with a narrow and vertical white band running from forehead to upper lip. Coat on upperparts is grizzled dark olive-green, underparts and legs are black. Tail is rather thickened and tipped with a black, bushy tassel.

Similar White facial stripe separates it from other monkeys in region; see local race of Sykes's monkey. Very restricted range.

Habitat Occupies montane forest in region, up to 4 600 m, as well as lowland and bamboo forest.

Behaviour Live in small troops of fewer than 10 individuals, each led by a single adult male. They forage in the trees, but also spend a lot of time on the ground. Are said also to be partly nocturnal, but have not been studied in the wild so this has not been verified.

These guenons have glands on the chest that are used for scent-marking branches within the troop territory.

Food Mixed diet that includes fruits, leaves and insects.

Reproduction In Democratic Republic of Congo births are said to take place between May and October. Apart from having single young, nothing else is known.

Longevity Up to 33 years in captivity.

Calls A loud 'boom' call; quiet twittering.

Occurrence Occur only in montane forests of region, on slopes of the Kigezi volcanoes in northern Rwanda and perhaps marginally into adjacent Uganda. Rare and possibly threatened within regional range. Apart from habitat loss, as with other primates they are probably threatened by the ever-growing bushmeat market.

MEASUREMENTS
Weight: 2.8–5.5 kg
Total length: 1.1 m (tail about half of total length)

RED-TAILED GUENON

Cercopithecus ascanius

Swahili: *Nkunga* **German:** *Rotschwanz-Weißnasenmeerkatze* **French:** *Cercopithèque ascagne*

Identification pointers Relatively small size. At least middle to tip of tail rufous-red, and nose usually white. Cheeks with longish, white hair and black streak. Face dark with blue around eyes. Upperparts dark greenish-olive with a reddish infusion; underparts usually white.

Similar Mixes with a number of other monkey species but should not be confused with other species in region.

Habitat Primary and secondary lowland and montane forest to about 2 000 m above sea level, also riverine and swamp forest, as well as acacia woodland where it adjoins forest.

Behaviour Diurnal and arboreal, only infrequently descending to the ground. Said to be active mainly during early morning and late afternoon, but can be observed at most times of the day. Troop size may vary from 7–35 individuals, and much larger concentrations may gather at an abundant food source. Usually each troop has a single adult male but sometimes more. Red-tails commonly mix with troops of monkeys of other species. Use all forest levels when foraging, but more than half the time is spent in middle strata.

Food Fruits and other plant parts, including resin; animal prey consists mainly of insects. When fruits are scarce, they eat more leaves.

Reproduction Single young born after unknown gestation, probably 125 days. Births recorded throughout the year, with distinct peak May to September.

Longevity 22.5 years in captivity.

Calls Fairly loud, explosive cough uttered by male as alarm; bird-like chirping and twittering between troop members.

Occurrence Occur in many forests of southern Uganda and in protected areas such as Mahali, Gombe (Tanzania); Mt Elgon, Kakamega, Masai Mara (Kenya).

MEASUREMENTS
Weight: ♂ 3–6 kg; ♀ 1.8–4 kg
Total length: ♂ 1–1.5 m;
♀ 85 cm–1.3 m
Tail length: 55–95 cm

PATAS MONKEY

Erythrocebus patas

Swahili: – **German:** *Husarenaffe* **French:** *Patas*

Identification pointers Distinctive long legs, slender body, greyhound-like appearance; largely terrestrial lifestyle. Upperparts brick red to yellowish-orange; underparts pale greyish-white. Grey grizzled hair on upperparts of arms. White moustache contrasts with usually darker face. Male larger, with blue scrotum.

Similar Highly distinctive; resembles no other monkey in East Africa; see savanna baboon with its 'broken' tail, long muzzle, and darker, uniform coat colour.

Habitat Dry savanna (especially with acacias) and rocky areas; dense cover.

Behaviour Sleep in trees but otherwise spend most of their time on the ground. The fastest of all primates – have been recorded at speeds of 55 kph. Troops usually made up of females, young and 1 dominant adult male, with solitary males quite common. Size of troops in East Africa ranges from 5–35 (rarely 50). Females defend territorial ranges against incursions by other individuals and troops. Males are very vigilant and frequently stand on hind legs or on raised ground seeking out predators and other males.

Food Fruits, seeds, leaves and some animal prey, especially insects, lizards and eggs of ground-nesting birds.

Reproduction Single young dropped after about 170-day gestation. Mating takes place during the rains, and births occur between January and May.

Longevity At least 21 years.

Calls Not as vocal as most other monkeys. Male will bark at other males. A two-phase bark and low, chattering alarm calls. Within troop, various hoots, chirrups, whistles and a deep cough.

Occurrence Fairly limited range in region; found in Murchison Falls; Kidepo (Uganda) and Masai Mara/Serengeti complex, as well as Tsavo (Kenya). Probably secure in these areas.

MEASUREMENTS
Weight: ♂ 10–18 kg (up to 23 kg recorded); ♀ 7–13 kg (few weights on record in East Africa)
Total length: ♂ 1.1–1.6 m; ♀ 1–1.5 m
Tail length: 50–74 cm

GREY-CHEEKED MANGABEY
Cercocebus (Lophocebus) albigenia

Swahili: – German: *Grauwangen-Mangabe* French: *Cercocèbe à joues grises*

Identification pointers A slender and somewhat elongated body, with the long tail often held erect, or curved over the back, especially when on the move. Snout longer than in other long-tailed monkeys. Overall blackish-brown coat colour with a pale grey-brown (dark brown in some races) mantle of long hair on the shoulders. Distinctive tuft of stiff hairs above each eye separates it from any other monkey in region. Longish hair on cheeks is grey. Tail quite long-haired but shorter towards tip.

Similar Should not be confused with other long-tailed monkeys in region, but see other forest species; tail posture distinctive.

Habitat Will occupy a wide range of forest types, including those of secondary growth and swamp forest up to 1 700 m.

Behaviour Mainly arboreal and will utilise all forest layers, but tend to favour the middle and upper reaches. Although seldom seen on the ground, in Uganda they have been recorded crossing open ground to raid crops. Troops average 15 individuals (up to 40) and may have 1 adult male, or several. They will commonly mix with other forest monkeys and guenons.

Food Feed on a variety of fruits and seeds, especially figs, and smaller quantities of leaves, flowers and small animal prey.

Reproduction A single young is dropped after about 180-day gestation. In Uganda most young are said to be born in May, but births have been recorded in other months.

Longevity Up to 20 years but >32 years in one captive animal.

Calls Loud, far-carrying 'whoop-gobble', also described as a bubbling croak.

Occurrence Occur in several Ugandan forests, including Bwamba, Kibale and Mabira.

MEASUREMENTS
Weight: ♂ 12–13 kg;
♀ 5.4–5.8 kg
Total length: ♂ 1.2–1.5 m;
♀ 1.2–1.3 m
Tail length: ♂ 75–88 cm;
♀ 67–77 cm

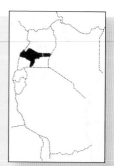

ZANZIBAR RED COLOBUS

Piliocolobus kirkii

Swahili: *Punju, Kima mweupe* **German:** *Sansibar-Stummelaffe* **French:** *Colobe bai de Zanzibar*

Identification pointers One of 4 species of red colobus in East Africa. Only found on Unguja (Zanzibar) and easily seen by visitors. Long-haired, with white brow-line. Has white cheek tufts contrasting with black face, underparts and much of hind limbs. Black on shoulders, with red hair on rest of back; paler tail. Pink on lips and nose.

Similar Very distinct from only other monkey on the island, Sykes's monkey.

Habitat Coastal thickets, coral rag thicket mainly in association with Jozani Forest, but at other locations too. Also in vicinity of agricultural land and stands of mangroves.

Behaviour Troops number from 30–50 individuals, each with up to 4 adult males, and there is much interaction within the group, such as grooming sessions. Males born into a troop remain with it, but females emigrate to other troops. Territories of troops tend to be rather small and although much time is spent in trees, they commonly come to the ground to forage. Also seek out charcoal on the ground, which they eat. It is believed this aids digestion and helps detoxify substances in their largely leaf-based diet.

Food Feed mainly on young and mature leaves, with smaller quantities of flowers and fruit.

Reproduction Single young can apparently be born at any time of year, but there may be a seasonal peak.

Longevity Not known. Rarely kept in captivity.

Calls Males have sneezing, high-pitched *chist* bark as well as brief growl; troop call is *nyow*.

Occurrence Considered endangered, with only about 1 500 individuals remaining. On Unguja (Zanzibar) main population centred around Jozani Forest.

MEASUREMENTS
Weight: ♂ 9–13 kg; ♀ 7–9 kg
Total length: 1–1.4 m
Tail length: 60–80 cm

Front

Back

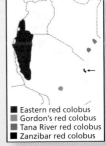

| ■ Eastern red colobus |
| ■ Gordon's red colobus |
| ■ Tana River red colobus |
| ■ Zanzibar red colobus |

GUEREZA (ABYSSINIAN) BLACK & WHITE COLOBUS *Colobus guereza*

Swahili: *Mbega, Kuluzu* **German:** *Guereza, Mantelaffe* **French:** *Colobe guéréza*

Identification pointers Overall black colour with mantle of long, white hair around sides and lower back in u-shape. Tail black to grizzled towards the base, with remainder white and bushy. In some races, white tail is impressively bushy. White brow-line, cheeks and short beard, with contrasting black cap and face. Newborns are white with pink face.

Similar Can only be confused with Angola black and white colobus in few places where ranges come close together, though latter have less extensive white mantle and less white hair on tail.

Habitat Occupies forests of many types, from sea level to at least 3 000 m, as well as dense woodland and riverine forest.

Behaviour Average troop size is 7–11 individuals, occasionally more, with either 1 adult male or, more rarely, 2 or more. Troops are strongly territorial and will chase trespassing troops from their core area. In early morning they sun-bask high in trees, looking somewhat like large blossoms. Spend most of their time in trees; will forage on the ground. Average troop home range usually less than 15 ha.

Food Mainly leaves, but some fruits. In some areas the bulk of their food may come from just 1 or 2 tree species.

Reproduction Single, all-white young, 450 g, after about 180 days (some give 140 days). No specific birth season.

Longevity At least 22 years.

Calls Low-pitched, far-carrying roar or croak. All troop members produce an impressive chorus in this way, usually answered by neighbouring troops.

Occurrence Although extensively hunted in the past, today they are commonly seen in a number of parks: Queen Elizabeth, Murchison Falls (Uganda); Lake Nakuru, Mt Kenya, Aberdares (Kenya); Serengeti, Ngorongoro, Mt Kilimanjaro, Arusha (Tanzania).

MEASUREMENTS
Weight: ♂ 13–23 kg
(rarely more than 18 kg);
♀ 8–9 kg
Total length: 1–1.6 m
Tail length: 65–90 cm

Front

Back

ANGOLA BLACK AND WHITE COLOBUS

Colobus angolensis

Swahili: *Mbega* **German:** *Angola-Stummelaffe* **French:** *Colobe blanc et noir d'Angola*

Identification pointers Black, glossy coat, with long white hair patches on shoulders, and white cheek patches. Tail usually black from base to at least midway, with longer white hair towards tip. Narrow white brow-band on forehead. Young initially with white coat.

Similar Guereza similar, but white mantle and bushy white tail are more extensive in that animal.

Habitat Primary and secondary forest at both low and high altitudes (to 3 000 m).

Behaviour Usually observed in highest forest strata, but do occasionally come to the ground to feed. Troops number 2–16 but up to 50; a troop sighted in Rwanda numbered 300. Troop structure variable and may include an adult male, or up to 5. Home ranges usually cover an average of 400 ha and each troop defends a territory. If threatened by a predator, the dominant troop male jumps up and down and gives vent to impressive roars. This continues until the rest of the troop has fled. This colobus frequently associates with other monkeys, guenons and mangabeys.

Food Seeds, young leaves and unripe fruits make up much of diet.

Reproduction Probably breed in all months in East Africa, but in parts of their range most young are born May to December. Single all-white young born after gestation of about 180 days.

Longevity Probably more than 20 years.

Calls Far-carrying roar or croak, similar to that of guereza.

Occurrence May have been a few local extinctions, but still quite common. Ruwenzori (Uganda); Mahale, Gombe, Mikumi (Tanzania).

MEASUREMENTS
Weight: ♂ 9–10 kg (probably heavier); ♀ 7–9 kg
Total length: 1.2–1.6 m
Tail length: 62–92 cm

Front

Back

COMMON CHIMPANZEE

Pan troglodytes

Swahili: *Soko mtu* **German:** *Schimpanse* **French:** *Chimpanzé*

Identification pointers Human-like, with large build and no tail. Hair black, as is usually the skin. In younger animals face and hands flesh-coloured . Youngsters have tuft of longish white hair on rump. Legs shorter than arms, so when walking back slopes downwards to rump.

Similar Gorillas larger and in proximity only in extreme south-west Uganda. Baboons lighter in colour, with longish tail.

Habitat Range of forest and woodland types, including wooded savanna usually adjacent to small evergreen forest patches in gorges and gullies. To altitudes of about 3 000 m above sea level.

Behaviour Loose communities of 15–>100 individuals, averaging 35. Each community's home range 10–50 km². Spend much time foraging on the ground and in trees, in small groups, or just a female and her young. Adult males in groups patrol the community's boundaries. At night, sleep in self-constructed tree nest.

Food Varied. Includes fruits, seeds, flowers, leaves, as well as insects, lizards, birds and other mammals. Males, particularly, hunt larger prey such as small antelope, monkeys and guenons.

Reproduction Promiscuous, with oestrous females mating with several males. Single young (very rarely twins) of 1.5–2 kg born after about 240 days.

Longevity 53 years recorded.

Calls Wide range of calls, including grunts, barks, squeals, whimpers and whoops, but far-carrying 'pant-hoot' is best known.

Occurrence Several protected populations, including Murchison Falls, Queen Elizabeth, Budongo, Kibale (Uganda); Mahale, Gombe (Tanzania). Numbers in Uganda probably about 5 000, in Tanzania 2 500. Small populations survive in Rwanda (Nyungwe Forest) and Burundi (Kibira, Rumango-Bururi).

MEASUREMENTS
Weight: ♂ 40–60 kg;
♀ 30–47 kg
Total length: 65–95 cm
Shoulder height: about 1 m

Back

190 mm

MOUNTAIN GORILLA

Gorilla gorilla beringei

Swahili: *Makaku* **German:** *Berggorilla* **French:** *Gorille de montagnes*

Identification pointers Largest primate in the region with massive build. Entirely black except mature males, which have silver-coloured saddle. Arms longer than legs and back slopes downwards from shoulders to rump. No tail.
Similar See chimpanzee, although the latter is much smaller.
Habitat Forest margins, secondary forest, vegetated clearings as well as bamboo thickets. Recorded at altitudes of up to 3 900 m.
Behaviour Live in groups of 2–37 individuals, each group dominated by an adult male silverback. Females and young construct sleeping nests in trees, but the heavy males usually bed down on the ground. Groups feed almost entirely on the ground, spending about a quarter of each day in this pursuit, and resting for much of remainder. Some seasonal movements related to food quality and availability.

Seldom move more than 1 km each day when foraging. Both males and females leave birth troop on reaching maturity, females joining lone males or small groups, while males remain alone until able to attract females and hold their own troop. Groups occupy home ranges of 5–35 km².
Food Wide range of herb, shrub and vine leaves, as well as plant pith.
Reproduction Young born at any time of year. Single infant of about 2 kg dropped after 260-day gestation.
Longevity 40–50 years.
Calls Hooting, low 'belch', soft grunting, roaring. Also beat chest with flat of hands to make far-carrying sound (adult males especially).
Occurrence Bwindi (Uganda). Some 320 survive here, just under half of world's population. Virunga (Rwanda and neighbouring Congo) holds about 380.

MEASUREMENTS
Weight: ♂ 160 kg; ♀ 95 kg
Standing height: ♂ 1.7 m; ♀ 1.5 m

Front

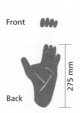

275 mm

Back

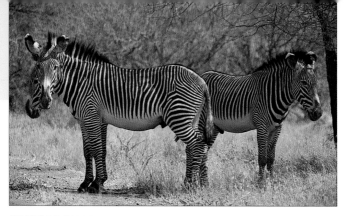

GREVY'S ZEBRA

Equus grevyi

Swahili: *Punda milia kubwa* **German:** *Grevyzebra* **French:** *Zèbre de Grévy*

Identification pointers Largest zebra, with narrow black striping on white background, no shadow stripes; underparts white. Broad dark stripe running along spine, bordered with white on rump. Long, mule-like ears and long, erect mane that runs from top of head to back of shoulders.

Similar Plains zebra smaller, stockier, with shorter ears, different stripe pattern and no dark dorsal stripe.

Habitat Occupies semi-desert plains and dry, open woodland savanna on flats as well as in broken hill country.

Behaviour Arid nature of their favoured habitats requires that they occupy vast home ranges (10 000 km² in some cases). Breeding stallions establish small core territories, which they mark with dung piles, close to a water source that is defended vigorously against other stallions. Herds of mares and young pass freely through these territories. During dry season herds of mixed gender and mixed age commonly sighted. More dryland adapted than plains zebra, but must drink every 2–5 days.

Food Mainly grass-eaters but up to 30% of food made up of bush and tree leaves, especially during dry season.

Reproduction Most foals born at onset of rainy season, although births have been recorded in all months. Gestation is about 390 days and a single foal is dropped.

Longevity 22 years in captivity.

Calls Male has loud bray, ending with long strangled squeak.

Occurrence Endangered: fewer than 1 500 in Ethiopia; about 4 000 in Kenya; extinct in Somalia. Illegal hunting and habitat loss; once extensively hunted for their attractive hides. East Turkana, Samburu and Meru (Kenya).

MEASUREMENTS
Weight: 350–430 kg
Shoulder height: 1.5 m
Total length: 3.2–3.5 m
Tail length: 75 cm

Front

100 mm

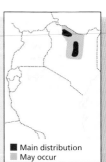

■ Main distribution
■ May occur

PLAINS ZEBRA

Equus burchellii

Swahili: *Punda milia* **German:** *Steppenzebra* **French:** *Zèbre de Burchell*

Identification pointers Stocky and pony-like, with black and white stripes that extend to underparts; East African races lack shadow stripes typically seen in southern African races. Mane stands erect (with hair-tufts alternately black and white and coinciding with stripes on neck), extending from top of head to shoulders. Tail short-haired near base; longer haired towards tip. Ears quite short.

Similar See taller Grevy's zebra, which has white underparts and large ears; overlap only in northern Kenya.

Habitat Open woodland and grassland savanna, from the coastal plain up to high-altitude grassland.

Behaviour Led by stallion, run in small family herds usually numbering 4–6 mares and their foals. Although much larger herds regularly seen, these stay together for only a short period and units retain their integrity. Stallions without mares join together in bachelor herds, or run alone. In many parts of East Africa, such as Serengeti and Tarangire, they are seasonal migrants. Frequently mix with other herding species, such as blue wildebeest, topi and gazelles. Access to water essential, as they need to drink every day. Heavily preyed on in some areas by lions, spotted hyaenas and wild dogs.

Food Grazers; browse rarely.

Reproduction Single foal weighing 30–35 kg born after 375-day gestation. Foaling coincides with onset of rainy season when there is abundant green grass.

Longevity 20 years; 40 years in captivity.

Calls Repeated barking *kwa-ha-ha*.

Occurrence Still common in several conservation areas. Ruaha, Ngorongoro, Serengeti, Tarangire, Selous, Mikumi (Tanzania); Tsavo, Samburu, Nairobi, Amboseli, Masai Mara, Lake Nakuru (Kenya). Largest populations in Serengeti/Masai Mara ecosystem.

MEASUREMENTS
Weight: 290–340 kg
Shoulder height: 1.3 m
Total length: 2.3–3 m
Tail length: 43–56 cm

Front

90 mm

HOOK-LIPPED (BLACK) RHINOCEROS

Diceros bicornis

Swahili: *Faru* **German:** *Spitzmaulnashorn* **French:** *Rhinocéros noir*

Identification pointers Characteristic large size, no hump on neck, pointed upper lip and 2 horns on face. When walking, head is held well above ground level. Often called 'black rhinoceros' but only appear this colour when wet or having rolled in fresh mud; usually varying shades of grey.

Similar See larger square-lipped rhinoceros with hump on shoulders and large head held close to ground when walking.

Habitat Areas of woodland, usually to an average height of 4 m, with access to water.

Behaviour Solitary, although several animals may congregate at a waterhole. During the day they usually lie up in dense cover and are seldom seen. Bulls and cows usually come together only to mate. Calf accompanies its mother until it is 2–4 years old. Individuals live in established home ranges that may overlap those of several individuals. Bulls establish dominance hierarchy by fighting each other but do not hold true territories. Have a reputation for aggression but this is often overstated.

Food Browse forms bulk of diet, but very selective in what they eat. Green grass eaten in varying quantities, as are various wild fruits. Twigs neatly bitten off by sharp-edged cheek-teeth.

Reproduction Calves weigh about 40 kg at birth, after gestation of some 450 days. Calf walks beside or behind mother. No birth season.

Longevity 40 years.

Calls Snort, wheeze, squeal, grunt and high-pitched scream, but often quiet.

Occurrence Brought to verge of extinction in East Africa, but a few well-protected populations are now secure. Extinct in Uganda, but about 650 individuals survive in Kenya and Tanzania. Tsavo, Nairobi, Lake Nakuru, Masai Mara (Kenya); Ngorongoro, Serengeti, Selous (Tanzania).

MEASUREMENTS
Weight: 800–1 100 kg
Shoulder height: 1.6 m
Total length: 3.5–4.3 m
Tail length: 70 cm
Record front horn length (EA): 1.36 m

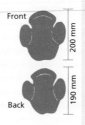

Front

200 mm

190 mm

Back

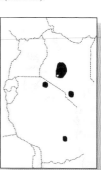

SQUARE-LIPPED (WHITE) RHINOCEROS *Ceratotherium simum*

Swahili: *Kifaru ya majani* **German:** *Breitmaulnashorn* **French:** *Rhinocéros blanc*

Identification pointers Large size (second only to elephant), with massive, square-muzzled head always held close to ground. Diagnostic are obvious hump located on shoulder, large pointed ears and 2 horns on front of face. Name 'white' (from Dutch word for 'wide', a reference to the broad mouth) is unfortunate as rarely are they this colour, usually taking on the colour of the mud in which they frequently wallow.
Similar Hook-lipped rhinoceros smaller, with pointed, not square, upper lip, and usually differ in habitat choice.
Habitat Preference shown for short-grass savanna, with areas of thick bush to provide cover and proximity to water for drinking and wallowing.
Behaviour Often seen in loosely knit groups and more social than hook-lipped rhinoceros. Dominant bull in group tolerates other bulls as long as they remain subservient. Cows occupy home

ranges covering 6–20 km² that may overlap territories of several bulls. Bulls leave large dung middens to mark edge of territory. Shade sought out during hotter hours of day, with most feeding in morning, evening and night hours. Despite their bulk, can reach top speed of 40 kph.
Food Selective grazers, preferring short grass species.
Reproduction After gestation of some 480 days, single calf weighing about 40 kg is dropped. Remains with mother for 2–3 years; always walks or runs in front of her.
Longevity 40–50 years.
Calls Rumbling growl and deep bellowing threat, panting call, squeal and whine, wail and chirping. Most occur when in contact with another rhinoceros.
Occurrence Northern race *C. s. cottoni* extinct in East Africa. Animals now present are from southern Africa (*C. s. simum*) and only in Kenya: Nakuru and private parks such as Solio.

MEASUREMENTS
Weight: ♂ 2 000–2 300 kg; ♀ 1 400–1 600 kg
Shoulder height: 1.8 m
Total length: 4.5–4.8 m
Tail length: 1 m
Record front horn length: (*C. s. cottoni*) over 1.27 m

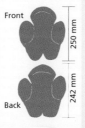

Front 250 mm
Back 242 mm

COMMON HIPPOPOTAMUS

Hippopotamus amphibius

Swahili: *Kiboko* **German:** *Flusspferd* **French:** *Hippopotame*

Identification pointers Large, barrel-shaped body with short, thick legs and massive head with broad muzzle. Skin smooth, hairless and overall greyish-black in colour with pinkish tinge at skin folds and around eyes, ears and mouth. Underparts paler greyish-pink. Tail short and flattened, with tuft of black bristles at tip.

Similar No similar species in region.

Habitat Preference for permanent waters (such as rivers, lakes, marshes and dams with sandy bottoms) adjacent to grazing grounds.

Behaviour Semi-aquatic, spending most daylight hours in water or basking on adjacent sand/mud banks. At night move to grazing grounds a few hundred metres to several kilometres from water. Herds usually number 10–15, although larger groups and solitary bulls not uncommon. Each herd dominated by a bull, and he vigorously repels other adult bulls. Herd bulls mark territories with dung scattered by flicking the tail. One of East Africa's most dangerous mammals.

Food A selective grazer, preferring shorter grasses.

Reproduction Mating takes place in the water. A single calf (25–55 kg) is dropped on land, in dense cover, after a gestation of 225–257 days. A double birth-peak in the region. (Well documented in Uganda, where it occurs in April and October.)

Longevity To 61 years in captivity, possibly also in wild.

Calls Deep roaring grunts in sequence, snorts, tusk gnashing.

Occurrence Decreased population in some areas but still common in parts of East Africa. Found in most parks with suitable rivers or waterbodies: Tsavo, Lake Turkana, Masai Mara, Meru (Kenya); Queen Elizabeth, Murchison (Uganda); Ngorongoro, Serengeti, Ruaha, Selous (Tanzania).

MEASUREMENTS
Weight: ♂ 1 000–>2 000 kg;
♀ 1 000–1 700 kg
Shoulder height: 1.5 m
Total length: 3.4–4.2 m
Tail length: 30–50 cm
Record tusk length (EA):
    163.83 cm (Kenya)

Front

250 mm

210 mm

Back

COMMON WARTHOG

Phacochoerus africanus

Swahili: *Ngiri, Mbango* **German:** *Warzenschwein* **French:** *Phacochère*

Identification pointers Typical pig-like appearance. Grey, sparsely haired skin takes on colour of local mud in which they wallow. Mane of long, erectile hair on neck and back; tufts of pale-coloured whiskers along sides of face. Male has 2 pairs of prominent wart-like structures on face, females 1 pair. Canine teeth develop into long curved tusks beyond upper lip. Tail held erect when running.

Similar See bushpig, red river hog and giant forest hog. Somali warthog (*P. aethiopicus*) identical in appearance and found only in far north-eastern Kenya.

Habitat Open grass and woodland savanna from low to high altitudes (3 000 m), low and high rainfall regions.

Behaviour Diurnal, spending nights in burrows (often taken over from aardvark or porcupine and then modified). Will also lie up in road culverts. There are records of them feeding at night. Adult females form small sounders with their young, but adult boars are normally solitary, circulating sounders to seek out oestrous sows. Size of home range varies according to food availability and water.

Food Mainly grass and grass roots; also dig for bulbs and corms. Browse and eat fallen wild fruits. Rarely take animal food. Often kneel on front legs when feeding.

Reproduction Litters of 1–8 (but usually 2–4) piglets (480–850 g) born after 170-day gestation. Remain in, or close to, burrow for first 2 weeks. Can breed throughout year, but in most of region seasonal peaks occur at end of dry season or with early rains.

Longevity 17 years in captivity, but probably less in wild.

Calls Normally silent but will grunt, snuffle and squeal.

Occurrence Common over much of East Africa; present in nearly all national parks.

MEASUREMENTS
Weight: ♂ 60–105 kg;
♀ 45–70 kg
Shoulder height: 60–70 cm
Total length: 1.3–1.8 m
Tail length: 45 cm
Record tusk length (EA):
56.20 cm (Uganda)

Front

45 mm

■ Somali warthog

BUSHPIG

Potamochoerus larvatus

Swahili: *Nguruwe* **German:** *Buschschwein* **French:** *Potamochère*

Identification pointers Pig-like in appearance, well-haired and bristled body with longer mane of hair on neck and shoulders. Head rather long, usually with greyish-white facial mask in adults and ears often with terminal tuft. Overall colour greyish-brown to reddish-brown but variable. Piglets dark brown with pale longitudinal stripes along body. Tail held down when running.

Similar Warthog is sparsely haired and usually greyish with tail held erect when running; see red river hog and giant forest hog.

Habitat Dense bush cover required, whether forest, woodland or reedbeds.

Behaviour Mainly nocturnal but sometimes seen during the day in undisturbed areas. Live in sounders of 2–15 animals, sometimes more, usually each with dominant boar; other boars often solitary. Dominant boar and sow in sounder probably defend a resource territory and boar plays active role in raising and defending piglets. When foraging, will move into more open areas, sometimes in close proximity to warthogs.

Food True omnivores, eating wide range of plant food and fairly large quantity of animal food. Dig with snout for roots, bulbs and insects. Readily scavenge from carcasses of dead mammals. On some occasions, especially during drought, will attack sheep and goats. Can be serious nuisance in croplands, such as maize, sorghum, potatoes and groundnuts.

Reproduction Most litters seem to be dropped at end of dry season, or start of the rains. After gestation of about 120–130 days, usually 2–4 (up to 8) piglets born, each weighing some 750 g.

Longevity 12–15 years in the wild.

Calls Grunts, squeals.

Occurrence Generally common over much of its range and present in many national parks.

MEASUREMENTS
Weight: 46–115 kg
  (♂ larger than ♀)
Shoulder height: 55–88 cm
Total length: 1.3–1.7 m
Tail length: 38 cm
Record tusk length (EA):
  21.91 cm (Kilimanjaro)

Front

55 mm

Red river hog & bushpig
Bushpig only

RED RIVER HOG
Potamochoerus porcus

Swahili: *Nguruwe* **German:** *Pinselohrschwein, Flussschwein* **French:** *Potamochère*

Identification pointers General structure and build similar to bushpig, but overall coat colour bright brick red and hair shorter than that of bushpig (but longish on underparts). Narrow, short-haired, white vertebral stripe runs from neck and onto tail. Remainder of tail dark, with terminal tuft of bristles. Tufts of white facial whiskers and long tassels of white hair on ear tips are diagnostic.
Similar See giant forest hog, but that animal very dark coloured and larger; bushpig similar, but has longer hair, less prominent ear tassels and overlaps in region only in far western Ugandan forests.
Habitat Most forest types; rarely seen far from dense cover, except in forest clearings.
Behaviour Believed to be mainly nocturnal, but some diurnal activity when undisturbed. Sounder sizes average 10 individuals, but groups of up to 60 have been observed. Behaviour little studied, though probably similar to

bushpig. Sounders probably led by dominant boar and sow, with most sounder members related. As with bushpig, boars not attached to sounders are probably solitary or form loosely knit bachelor groups. Heavily hunted across much of its range; likely to be the same in western Uganda, except protected areas.
Food Mix of plant and animal food, former most important. Leathery but sensitive snout used to dig out roots, bulbs, insects and burrowing frogs.
Reproduction Believed to be seasonal breeders, but very little known about this aspect of their biology. Probably similar to that of bushpigs.
Longevity 12–15 years.
Calls Range of grunts and squeals.
Occurrence Limited distribution in East Africa but probably not threatened. Said to be present in Queen Elizabeth, Ruwenzori, Bwindi (Uganda).

MEASUREMENTS
Weight: 45–80 kg;
  (♂ larger than ♀)
Shoulder height: 50–90 cm
Total length: 1.2–1.7 m
Tail length: 36 cm

Front

55 mm

■ Red river hog & bushpig
■ Bushpig only

35

GIANT FOREST HOG

Hylochoerus meinertzhageni

Swahili: *Nguruwe nyeusi* **German:** *Riesenwaldschwein* **French:** *Hylochère*

Identification pointers Largest wild pig in East Africa (and in the world), with powerful build. Body covered with coarse, black hair. Head elongated and massive, with large, swollen protrusions between eyes and tusks – particularly well developed in boars. Longer bristly hairs usually present on top of head. Tusks long, protruding well beyond upper lip, especially in boars. Thin, tufted tail held down when running.

Similar Size and colour separate it from bushpig, red river hog and warthog.

Habitat Wide range of forest types, from lowland to highland (3 800 m), as well as dense thickets and woodland. Feeds in open grassland adjacent to dense thickets. Needs regular access to water.

Behaviour Diurnal and nocturnal, living in sounders of 6–14 individuals led by dominant boar. Home ranges of sounders believed to average 10 km², but will vary according to local conditions. Typical home range will include regularly used resting sites, a network of radiating paths, waterhole, mineral licks and communal dung middens. Spend up to 10 hours each day feeding.

Food Mainly graze, but also eat range of other plants and sometimes small animals.

Reproduction Litters may be dropped at any time of year, but there are distinct peaks. Gestation some 151 days, with 2–4 piglets per litter. All East African wild pigs, except warthogs, usually drop young in 'haystack' of grass collected by sow.

Longevity Not known, but probably similar to bushpig and red river hog.

Calls Grunts and squeals.

Occurrence Limited range in East Africa, declining in some areas. In the Aberdares, reintroduction of lions greatly reduced the population (lions have since been removed). Aberdares, Mt Kenya, Mt Elgon, Kakamega (Kenya); Queen Elizabeth, Budongo, Murchison (Uganda).

MEASUREMENTS
Weight: 130–235 kg
(♂ much larger than ♀)
Shoulder height: 85 cm–>1 m
Total length: 1.6–2.5 m
Tail length: 30–45 cm
Record tusk length (EA):
  39.37 cm (Semliki, Uganda)

Front

65 mm

DROMEDARY

Camelus dromedarius

Swahili: – **German:** *Dromedar* **French:** *Dromadaire*

Identification pointers Cannot be mistaken for any other species in region. Its size, long neck and legs, and large hump on the back are characteristic. Considerable variation in colour, but most animals are shades of brown or grey-brown. Superbly adapted to desert, with large, rounded feet, nostrils that can close and ability to survive long periods without water.

Similar Cannot be confused, but see larger, distinctly marked giraffe.

Habitat Desert and semi-desert with both sandy and rocky substrate.

Behaviour Frequently seen roaming in more arid areas of Kenya as a domestic or feral animal. Left to their own devices, camels may form bachelor herds, or herds of females with calves. A single dominant bull controls all groups, but an old female often leads the herd.

Food Takes both browse and grass from wide range of plants. Even plants with high salt content that are rejected by other herbivores are readily eaten.

Reproduction Mating in the region takes place April to June and September to November. This can be influenced by climatic conditions, and single young (rarely twins) are dropped after about 12-month gestation. Birth weight averages 37 kg.

Longevity Up to 50 years but usually less.

Calls A repertoire of growls, snarls, gurgles, grumbles and squeals.

Occurrence Large numbers held in captivity and semi-feral state in Kenya. The dromedary was first domesticated as long ago as 4 000 BC, probably in Arabia. Fossil remains indicate that as a wild animal it also occurred in Africa.

MEASUREMENTS
Weight: 300–900 kg
  (♂ heavier than ♀)
Shoulder height: 1.8–2.3 m
Total length: 2.8–3.5 m
Tail length: 35–55 cm

Front

220 mm

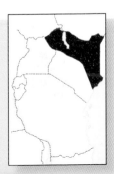

GIRAFFE

Giraffa camelopardalis

Swahili: *Twiga* **German:** *Giraffe* **French:** *Girafe*

Identification pointers Unmistakable with its immense height, long legs and neck, and back sloping downwards from shoulders to rump. Body covered with lattice pattern of large, irregularly shaded patches separated by networks of light-coloured bands. Both sexes carry pair of short, blunt horns. In East Africa there are 3 distinct races. Southern Kenya and all of Tanzania: Maasai (*G .c. tippelskirchi* ); northern Kenya: reticulated (*G .c. reticulata* ); north-east Uganda and introduced to Lake Nakuru area (Kenya): remnant populations of Rothschild's (*G. c. rothschildi* ). Some see these races as full species. See photographs.

Similar Unmistakable.

Habitat Dry savanna woodland, particularly in areas dominated by *Acacia, Commiphora, Combretum* and *Terminalia* trees. Access to drinking water essential.

Behaviour Do not occupy defended territories; move in large home ranges of 20->120 km². Usually herds of 4–30, but groups unstable; much intermingling of herds. Adult bulls generally solitary. Feed by day and at night; rest during hottest hours. At full gallop can sustain 60 kph.

Food Almost exclusively browsers; take leaves, also flowers, shoots, rarely pods.

Reproduction Single calf, averaging 100 kg, after about 450-days' gestation; calf stands and walks within 1 hour.

Longevity Up to 28 years.

Calls Seldom heard; rarely bray (when under stress), grunt and bellow.

Occurrence Arusha, Ngorongoro, Serengeti, Kilimanjaro, Selous, Katavi (Tanzania); Tsavo, Samburu, Lake Nakuru, Masai Mara, Meru, Nairobi (Kenya); Kidepo, Murchison Falls (Uganda). Common in many savanna areas; hunting and habitat destruction have reduced their range.

MEASUREMENTS

Weight: ♂ 970–1 400 kg; 700–950 kg

Shoulder height: ♂ 2.6–3.5 m; ♀ 2–3 m

Total height: ♂ 3.9–5.2 m; ♀ 3.7–4.7 m

Total length: 4.6–5.7 m; ♀ <5 m

Tail length: ♂ 96 cm–1.5 m; ♀ 75–90 cm

Front

180 mm

AFRICAN BUFFALO

Syncerus caffer

Swahili: *Nyati, Mbogo* **German:** *Afrikanischer Büffel* **French:** *Buffle d'Afrique*

Identification pointers Cattle-like appearance, but easily separated from domestic cattle. Massive size, heavily built; short, stocky legs and large, fringed ears that hang below horns. Massive horns form heavy boss where they meet, tips pointing inwards. Overall colour dark brown to black, without markings. Some in far western Uganda reddish-brown.

Similar Can only be confused with similarly coloured domestic cattle, but see horns. Dwarf, or forest, buffalo may have hybridised in far western Ugandan forests and adjacent DRC (Congo).

Habitat Open woodland savanna with abundant grass and drinking water. In some areas (such as on Mt Kenya) occupy mountain forest, feeding in open glades.

Behaviour Run in herds of several score to several thousand individuals, but also common are solitary and small groups of bulls. Mixed herds consist of cows, young of different ages and adult bulls maintaining a dominance hierarchy. Cows also establish pecking order among themselves. Herds occupy defined home ranges. Much feeding done at night; seek out shade during hottest hours. Usually drink in early morning and late afternoon.

Food Mainly grazers, preferring grasses that grow in dense swards. Some browse is taken, mainly in dry season.

Reproduction Most calves born in warm, wet seasons when food supply reliable. Single calf, about 40 kg at birth, dropped after some 340-days' gestation.

Longevity 20 years wild; 26 in captivity.

Calls Bellow, bleat (calf), 'creaking gate' call, *maaa* (similar to cow *moo*), low grunts and croaks.

Occurrence In most major parks and reserves. Has lost much East African range to cattle ranching, agriculture and habitat destruction; still common/ abundant in many areas.

MEASUREMENTS
Weight: ♂ 700 kg; ♀ 550 kg
Shoulder height: 1.4 m
Total length: 2.9 m
Tail length: >70 cm
Record horn length (EA):
127.32 cm (Lake Manyara)

Front

120 mm

■ African buffalo
■ Transition with forest buffalo

COMMON ELAND
Tragelaphus oryx

Swahili: *Pofu, Mbunju* **German:** *Elenantilope, Eland* **French:** *Eland du Cap*

Identification pointers Largest antelope in the region, with ox-like appearance. Overall coloration is fawn to tawny-grey, with older animals often more grey on the forequarters, neck and face. Many animals have some white striping, but often indistinct. Bulls develop large, pendulous dewlap on throat and lower neck, and prominent hair tuft is located on the face. Both sexes carry horns, with those of bulls being heavier.

Similar Size and coloration separate them from other species, but see roan and greater kudu.

Habitat Occupies most savanna and open woodland associations, from semi-desert to high-rainfall areas. Recorded to 5 000 m above sea level on Kilimanjaro.

Behaviour Usually form herds of 25–60 animals (sometimes much larger); often highly nomadic. In an East African study, herd home ranges covered as much as 1 500 km² for mixed herds, much smaller for adult bulls. Bulls establish hierarchy that determines mating rights. Active night and day.

Food Mainly browsers but do graze, especially on green grass. In arid areas they dig with front hooves for bulbs, corms and roots. Use horns to break branches for access to leaves.

Reproduction After gestation of about 270 days, single calf (rarely twins) weighing 22–36 kg may be dropped at any time of year – but in parts seasonal. Calf remains hidden for first 2 weeks.

Longevity 20 years; 26 in captivity.

Calls Bleat, loud alarm bark.

Occurrence Ruaha, Ngorongoro, Serengeti, Selous (Tanzania); Tsavo, Masai Mara, Samburu, Meru, Amboseli, Nairobi (Kenya); Kidepo (Uganda). Once widespread in East Africa, but range has shrunk considerably. Present in most savanna parks.

MEASUREMENTS
Weight: ♂ 700–900 kg; ♀ 450 kg
Shoulder height: ♂ 1.7 m; ♀ 1.5 m
Total length: ♂ 3–4.2 m; ♀ 2.2–3.5 m
Tail length: 60 cm
Record horn length (EA): 107 cm (Selous, Tanzania)

Front

100 mm

BONGO

Tragelaphus (Boocercus) euryceros

Swahili: *Bongo* **German:** *Bongo* **French:** *Bongo*

Identification pointers Large, stocky antelope; bright chestnut-coloured coat, with 10–16 vertical white stripes on each side. White chevron between eyes and usually 2 distinct white spots on each side of face. Contrasting black and white markings on legs. Short, erectile crest runs from shoulders to rump; bulls have black fringe on upper throat. Both sexes carry heavy, smooth and openly spiralled horns that are white-tipped. Ears are noticeably large.

Similar Bushbuck much smaller; bongo separated by habitat from the 2 kudu species and the sitatunga.

Habitat Dense lowland and montane forest, extending into bamboo thickets.

Behaviour Adult bulls believed to be mainly solitary, while cows and calves form loosely associated nursery herds. Home ranges quite large, with up to 300 km² recorded in the Aberdares, but usually smaller elsewhere. Territories

not held and bulls circulate over ranges of several nursery herds. Bulls rarely fight and rely on elaborate displays and posturing to intimidate each other.

Food Principally browsers, but do, on occasion, graze on green grass. Recorded feeding on wide range of plants, including bamboo, various creepers, tree leaves, flowers, fruits and fungi.

Reproduction Seasonal breeding peaks occur in the region; single calf, weighing approximately 22 kg, dropped after gestation of some 284 days.

Longevity 15–20 years, rarely 25 years.

Calls Grunt and snort; cow has mooing contact call with calf; alarm bleat.

Occurrence Mt Kenya, Aberdares (Kenya). Has disappeared from much of East African range and probably extinct in Uganda. Reintroduction of lions to the Aberdares resulted in drastic declines in numbers of this antelope.

MEASUREMENTS
Weight: ♂ 300 kg; ♀ 240 kg
Shoulder height: 1.25 m
Total length: 2.5–2.6 m
Tail length: 25–28 cm
Record horn length (EA):
 100.33 cm (Mt Kenya)

Front

♂

♀

GREATER KUDU

Tragelaphus strepsiceros

Swahili: *Tandala mKubwa* **German:** *Großer Kudu* **French:** *Grand koudou*

Identification pointers Large, with long legs and short-maned shoulder hump. Overall coat colour grey-brown to rufous, with neck usually greyer than rest of body. Flanks have 6–10 vertical stripes. Distinct, narrow white chevron between eyes. Bulls have fringe of long hair on throat and lower neck. Ears very large and rounded. Only the bull carries long, deeply spiralled horns, regarded as among the most spectacular of all antelope horns.

Similar Lesser kudu much smaller; separated from bongo and sitatunga by habitat.

Habitat Wooded savanna, especially acacia woodland and broken hill country.

Behaviour Herds generally small and average 3–10 individuals, usually cows and young. Larger groups may be seen, but these are temporary, at either water or favoured feeding areas. Bulls circulate freely throughout the year; normally only join nursery herds during the rut. Small bachelor herds common, but solitary bulls frequently seen. As with the common eland, very adept jumpers. Active at night and during the cooler daylight hours, resting under cover in the hottest hours.

Food Mainly browse, but will graze, especially when grass is green. During drought will eat tree bark, scraped off with their incisors. Seed pods, especially of acacia trees, readily taken, as are their blossoms.

Reproduction Single calf, weighing about 16 kg, born after 270-day gestation. No distinct birth season and calf remains hidden for first 2–3 months.

Longevity 7–8 years; 23 in captivity.

Calls Loud, gruff bark; other calls made but seldom heard.

Occurrence Ruaha, Tarangire, Katavi, Selous (Tanzania); Marsabit, Lake Bogoria, Lake Turkana (Kenya); Kidepo (Uganda). Reduced range; still quite widespread in Tanzania, more limited in Kenya, and only in north-east Uganda.

MEASUREMENTS
Weight: ♂ 250 kg; ♀ 180 kg
Shoulder height: 1.2–1.55 m
Total length: 2.3–2.9 m
Tail length: 43 cm
Record horn length (EA):
142.88 cm (Kilolo, Tanzania)

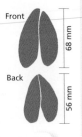

Front

68 mm

Back

56 mm

LESSER KUDU

Tragelaphus imberbis

Swahili: *Tandala ndogo* **German:** *Kleiner Kudu* **French:** *Petit koudou*

Identification pointers Medium size; body form similar to greater kudu. Overall coat colour greyish-brown, but females brighter. Up to 15 narrow, white vertical stripes down sides of body and 2 distinctive white markings on throat. Lower legs orange-brown in colour. Only the ram carries widely spiralled horns.

Similar Greater kudu much bigger and lacks white throat patches; separated from bongo and sitatunga by habitat.

Habitat Strong preference for areas dominated by acacia woodland and dense scrub, often receiving low rainfall. Rarely move far from cover and are difficult to observe.

Behaviour Occupy fixed home ranges (usually 2–3 km²) and do not form true herds. May live solitary life, or may be seen in pairs, or in small groups of ewes with their young. Neither ram nor ewe defends territory, but rams may live in fairly close proximity, rarely interacting and trying to avoid one another. Well camouflaged and easily overlooked. Independent of drinking water. Active predominantly at night and during cooler hours of day.

Food Mainly browse on leaves, flowers, fruits and seed pods, but also eat succulents and some grass during rainy season. Highly selective in choice of grass species and stage of grass growth.

Reproduction Although lambs born at any time of year, there is distinct peak during rainy season. Single calf, weighing about 7 kg, born after 220-day gestation.

Longevity 15 years in captivity.

Calls Bark most frequently heard.

Occurrence Ruaha, Tarangire (Tanzania); Tsavo, Meru, Samburu, Turkana (Kenya); Kidepo (Uganda). Nowhere common; numbers reduced in some areas through hunting but mainly habitat loss.

MEASUREMENTS
Weight: ♂ 100 kg; ♀ 62 kg
Shoulder height: 1 m
Total length: 1.85–2.05 m
Tail length: 25–30 cm
Record horn length (EA): 77.15 cm
  (Ngasserei, Tanzania)

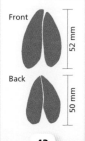

Front

52 mm

Back

50 mm

43

SITATUNGA
Tragelaphus spekei

Swahili: *Nzohe* **German:** *Sitatunga, Wasserkudu* **French:** *Sitatunga*

Identification pointers Medium-sized antelope; hindquarters higher than shoulders. Coat fairly long and shaggy. Ram overall reddish to grey-brown with few or no clear white markings; ewe more rufous with several distinct vertical white stripes. Ram carries long, white-tipped, lightly spiralled horns. Hoofs exceptionally long, an adaptation to their semi-aquatic life.

Similar Unlikely to be confused with other species, but see bushbuck; may feed at night in fringing woodland where smaller bushbuck often occur.

Habitat Dense reed beds and well-vegetated aquatic environments, but will feed at night in woodland fringing swamps. May be observed feeding on floating grass.

Behaviour Common grouping consists of adult ram with several ewes and their young. Solitary rams common, as are mixed groups of young animals. Most feeding takes place by day, but they also feed at night. Take readily to water to escape danger, or move between feeding sites, and they can swim well for long distances. Home ranges are small, this being a measure of the abundance and nutritional richness of their food.

Food Papyrus, reeds, aquatic grasses, as well as dryland grasses, but will also browse in adjacent forest and woodland.

Reproduction Single fawn dropped after about 220-day gestation. Fawn remains hidden for several weeks after birth. Seasonal birth-peaks in some areas; little known of peaks in East African range.

Longevity 17–20 years in captivity.

Calls Males have loud, frequent bark, heard especially at night.

Occurrence Queen Elizabeth (Uganda); Saiwa Swamp (Kenya). Populations very fragmented across their limited East African range.

MEASUREMENTS
Weight: ♂ 115 kg; ♀ 55 kg
Shoulder height: ♂ 88 cm–1.25 m; ♀ 75–90 cm
Total length: ♂ 1.72–1.95 m; ♀ 1.55–1.8 m
Tail length: 22 cm
Record horn length (EA): 82.23 cm (Uganda)

Front

120–180 mm

♂ ♀

BUSHBUCK

Tragelaphus scriptus

Swahili: *Mbawala, Pongo* **German:** *Buschbock* **French:** *Guib harnaché*

Identification pointers Smallest of spiral-horned antelope; overall coat colour varies from dark brown to reddish-yellow (and shades between). Vertical white stripes and spots on sides, but this is very variable. Has 2 white patches on throat. Several subspecies in region, but all should be recognised as bushbuck. Ram carries short, smooth, shallowly spiralled horns. Ram has erectile crest along back.

Similar Although differing in size and horns, see lesser kudu where ranges overlap.

Habitat Riverine woodland and bush cover associated with, or close to, water, from sea level to 3 000 m above sea level. Enters open glades, but rarely observed far from cover.

Behaviour Mainly solitary, but loosely knit groups of ewes and lambs commonly observed. In suitable habitat may reach amazingly high densities (according to a study, 26 in 1 km²). Home ranges overlap, but each adult has restricted area where it lies up. Although mainly nocturnal, frequently feed during cooler early morning and late afternoon hours.

Food Mainly browse on leaves, but also flowers, fruits and shoots; may eat grass and agricultural crops.

Reproduction Single fawn, weighing 3.5–4.5 kg, dropped after 180-day gestation. Up to first 4 months of life fawn lies up in dense cover. Birth-peaks coincide with rains.

Longevity >12 years in captivity.

Calls Main call a sharp bark.

Occurrence Selous, Ruaha, Tarangire, Katavi, Mahale, Gombe, Mikumi, Serengeti (Tanzania); Shimba Hills, Tsavo, Masai Mara, Nairobi, Mt Elgon, Kakamega, Aberdares, Mt Kenya (Kenya); Queen Elizabeth, Murchison Falls, Kidepo (Uganda). Has lost some ground to habitat destruction, but still common and widespread.

MEASUREMENTS
Weight: ♂ 45 kg; ♀ 30 kg
Shoulder height: ♂ 80 cm; ♀ 70 cm
Total length: ♂ 1.36–1.66 m
Tail length: 20 cm
Record horn length (EA): 48.90 cm (Mau Forest, Kenya)

Front

44 mm

BEISA ORYX

Oryx gazella beisa, O. g. callotis

Swahili: *Choroa* **German:** *Eritrea-Spießbock* **French:** *Oryx beisa*

Identification pointers Large, heavily built antelope with short, thick neck. Both sexes carry long, ringed, rapier-like horns. Horns of bull shorter and stouter than those of cow. Overall body colour sandy-fawn, sometimes with greyish tinge, and with distinctive black and white facial markings, narrow black stripe on sides, black throat/neck stripe and black ring on upper forelegs. Tail is horse-like, and race *O. g. callotis* has long tufts of black hair on ear tips. Races considered by some to be full species.

Similar Nothing similar in region, but see larger roan with scimitar-shaped horns, yet with similar black and white facial markings.

Habitat Dry, open country; also open woodland, grass savanna and sometimes hill country. Will drink; water not essential.

Behaviour Form herds of up to 30 individuals, but larger temporary groups come together. Some seasonal variation in herd size. Herds may be mixed, with bulls and nursery herds together, though nursery herds and bulls often solitary. Territorial bulls round up mixed or nursery herds, and these bulls have sole mating rights. Bulls ranging from 5–7 years of age hold territories for up to 3 years. Home ranges of herds may cover several hundred km², and are larger in more arid areas.

Food Mainly grazers, but will browse. Often take tree pods, especially acacia.

Reproduction Single calf dropped after some 264 days; joins herd only at 3–6 weeks. Births linked to seasonal rainfall.

Longevity 18–20 years in captivity.

Calls Bulls roar when fighting; contact grunt but otherwise silent.

Occurrence Tsavo (*O. g. callotis*), Samburu, Meru (*O. g. beisa*) (Kenya); Tarangire (*O. g. callotis*) (Tanzania). Declines across its range, but in a number of national parks.

MEASUREMENTS
Weight: ♂ 240 kg; ♀ 210 kg
Shoulder height: 1.2 m
Total length: 1.9–2.16 m
Tail length: 46 cm
Record horn lengths (EA):
O. g. beisa 105.09 cm;
O. g. callotis 110.17 cm
(Lake Magadi, Kenya)

Front

110 mm

■ *O. g. beisa*
■ *O. g. callotis*

ROAN ANTELOPE

Hippotragus equinus

Swahili: *Korongo* **German:** *Pferdeantilope* **French:** *Hippotrague*

Identification pointers Second largest antelope in region, after common eland. Horse-like, with short, thick neck and distinct erect mane running down from between ears to just beyond shoulders. Conspicuous black and white facial markings and long ears tipped with tassel of hair. Overall body colour greyish-brown; underparts paler. Both sexes carry back-curved and heavily ringed horns, those of bull being heavier.

Similar Sable antelope has longer horns and coloration differs; common eland is much bigger and its horns are straight.

Habitat Open or lightly wooded grassland with medium to tall grasses and access to water. Short grassed areas avoided.

Behaviour Herd size usually 5–12 individuals, each led by dominant bull. Bull defends nursery herd (not territory) against other bulls. Herd usually led by cow that dominates other cows and selects feeding and resting locations.

Young bulls driven from herds and form bachelor groups; only at 5–6 years do they seek out nursery herds. Larger herds occur, but are merely temporary gatherings, seldom stable. Mainly diurnal, but night activity not unusual, especially in areas where hunted.

Food Grazers, selecting medium-height and long grasses.

Reproduction Single calf, weighing 15–18 kg, dropped after about 280-day gestation. Births recorded throughout year, but peaks known. After birth, calf remains hidden for about 2 weeks, and is suckled by its mother twice daily.

Longevity 17 years in captivity.

Calls Snorts; cow and calf manifest bird-like contact and distress calls; bulls roar during fights.

Occurrence Ruaha, Tarangire, Serengeti (Tanzania); Kidepo (Uganda); Shimba Hills, Masai Mara (Kenya). Considerable losses in range and numbers.

MEASUREMENTS
Weight: 220–300 kg
(♂ heavier than ♀)
Shoulder height: 1.1–1.5 m
Total length: 2.26–2.89 m
Tail length: 54 cm
Record horn length (EA):
83.19 cm (Ikoma, Tanzania)

120 mm

SABLE ANTELOPE

Hippotragus niger

Swahili: *Palahala, Mbarapi* **German:** *Rappenantilope* **French:** *Hippotrague noir*

Identification pointers Large size, black and white facial markings and long, strongly ringed, sabre-like horns diagnostic. Adult bulls overall black, with contrasting white underparts. Cows usually reddish-brown to chestnut, often darkening with age; underparts white. Backs of ears in both sexes brown. Female horns similar to those of male, but shorter and more slender. Erect, fairly long mane from top of neck to just beyond shoulders.

Similar Roan antelope has shorter horns and different coloration.

Habitat Dry, open woodland with medium-length to tall grass; access to water needed.

Behaviour Usually live in herds of 10–30 individuals; larger temporary groups occasionally seen. Bulls establish territories that overlap home ranges of 1 or more nursery herds. These home ranges are stable and quite small. During the rut, bulls try to hold nursery herds within their territories.

Herds led by adult cow that usually directs movements to feeding and resting grounds. Young bulls join bachelor herds until their fifth or sixth year, then move away to establish own territories. Most activity early morning and late afternoon.

Food Mainly graze, but on occasion browse, especially in dry season.

Reproduction Seasonal breeding linked to rains, but Shimba Hills (Kenya) population said to be non-seasonal. Single calf, 13–18 kg, after gestation of about 270 days. Calf remains hidden for first few weeks and is moved to a new location after each suckling (twice daily).

Longevity 17 years in captivity.

Calls Cow and calf manifest bird-like contact and distress calls; bulls roar; both sexes snort.

Occurrence Probably some 30 000 in Tanzania; only 1 small population in Kenya. Ruaha, Selous (Tanzania); Shimba Hills (Kenya).

MEASUREMENTS
Weight: 180–270 kg
Shoulder height: 1.35 m
Total length: 2.3–2.56 m
Tail length: 50 cm
Record horn length (EA):
   121.60 cm (Tanzania)

115 mm

WATERBUCK

Kobus ellipsiprymnus

Swahili: *Kuru* **German:** *Wasserbock* **French:** *Cobe defassa, Cobe à croissant*

Identification pointers Quite large, with coarse and shaggy coat ranging from grey-brown to reddish in colour. The 2 races are very similar, but more common *K. e. ellipsiprymnus* has white ring around rump, while *K. e. defassa* has all-white rump. Only the bull carries long, ringed and forward-swept horns. White upper-throat band usually present in both races, with white around muzzle and on lips. Strong, distinctive smell.

Similar See reedbuck species, but they are all much smaller and lighter coloured, with bushy tails.

Habitat Always associated with water, preferring areas with reed beds or tall grass; also found in woodland. Graze in open grassland adjacent to cover.

Behaviour Usually in small herds of 5–10 individuals but up to 30. Larger herds usually seen during rainy season. Adult bulls establish territories through which nursery herds move freely, but during the rut they try to hold cows for mating. Bulls establish own territories at 5 or 6 years of age; once established these are stable and held until usurped by another bull.

Food Mainly grasses, but browse on occasion, especially in dry season.

Reproduction After about 280-day gestation, single (rarely twins) calf weighing some 13 kg is dropped. Calf remains hidden for first 3–5 weeks. Non-seasonal breeding nearest the equator, but more seasonal away from it.

Longevity 18 years in wild, but this is exceptional.

Calls Cow and calf bleat; alarm snort.

Occurrence Ngorongoro, Serengeti, Selous, Katavi, Tarangire, Ruaha, Mikumi (Tanzania); Masai Mara, Tsavo, Nairobi, Lake Nakuru (Kenya); Queen Elizabeth, Murchison Falls, Kidepo (Uganda). Wiped out in some areas, but still relatively common; meat not favoured by either hunter or poacher.

MEASUREMENTS
Weight: 250–270 kg
Shoulder height: 1.3 m
Total length: 2.1–2.74 m
Tail length: 35 cm
Record horn length (EA):
  K. e. ellipsiprymnus 93.98 cm;
  K. e. defassa 99.70 cm

Front

Back

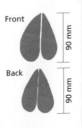

90 mm

90 mm

■ *K.e. defassa*
■ *K.e. ellipsiprymnus*

KOB

Kobus kob

Swahili: *Swala kob* **German:** *Kob* **French:** *Cobe*

Identification pointers Medium-sized antelope with overall rich reddish-brown coat, paler to white underparts, white throat patch, and rings around eyes. Only ram carries thick, heavily ringed, lyre-shaped horns. Rams more heavily built than ewes, with broad, powerful neck. Called 'Uganda kob' in region.

Similar Nothing similar in limited range and restricted habitat. See smaller bohor reedbuck, but they lack kob's distinct facial markings; horns are very different.

Habitat Floodplains and gently undulating country with good grass cover and proximity to water.

Behaviour Form nursery herds of 15–40 animals that are largely stable. Non-territorial rams form loosely attached bachelor herds. During dry season they form mixed herds numbering as many as 1 000 animals.

Adult rams hold small circular territories, with several adjoining each other known as leks. In areas of high density, these territories can be as small as 50 m². Ewes move freely through these territories; if a ewe is in breeding condition a ram will try to hold her briefly in his area for mating.

Food Almost exclusively grazers.

Reproduction Single fawn, weighing 4–5 kg, dropped after some 210 days. Young remain hidden for 6–8 weeks after birth. Breed throughout year in Uganda, but periods of breeding reduced during driest times.

Longevity 17 years in captivity.

Calls Distinct whistles; ewes bleat to calves.

Occurrence Queen Elizabeth, Murchison Falls (Uganda). Extinct in Tanzania and Kenya, with range greatly reduced in Uganda. Losses result mainly from hunting.

MEASUREMENTS
Weight: ♂ to 120 kg; ♀ 60 kg
Shoulder height: ♂ 92 cm; ♀ 78 cm
Total length: ♂ 1.65–2.2 m;
♀ 1.5–1.9 m
Tail length: ♂ 25–40 cm; ♀ 18–30 cm
Record horn length (EA): 69.22 cm
(Lolim, Uganda)

Front

67 mm

Back

62 mm

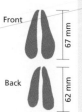

PUKU

Kobus vardoni

Swahili: *Swala puku* **German:** *Puku* **French:** *Puku*

Identification pointers Medium-sized antelope, with upperparts golden to yellow-brown, slightly paler sides and off-white underparts. Throat, sides of muzzle and hair around eyes also off-white. Otherwise no distinct markings. Legs uniformly brown. Well-haired tail golden-yellow with white hairs below. Only ram carries relatively short but stout, lyre-shaped and deeply ringed horns. Some authorities consider puku to be a subspecies of kob.

Similar See smaller bohor reedbuck with shorter, sharply forward-pointing horns of ram. Common reedbuck has distinct markings; horns differ. Also see impala (has distinguishing markings on rump). Kob and puku ranges do not overlap.

Habitat Open flatland adjacent to rivers and marshes, but rarely venturing far onto open floodplain.

Behaviour Herds of 5–30 individuals, but numbers unstable as movement of individuals commonly occurs between different groups. Nursery herds consisting of ewes and young move across territories of several rams. These territories are temporary; usually held for short periods, rarely longer than a few months. Rams attempt to keep nursery herds within their territories and mate with ewes in breeding condition.

Food Predominantly grasses.

Reproduction Single lamb, weighing about 5 kg, born after gestation of some 240 days. Lamb hides in a grass form for first few weeks of life. When lambs join herd they keep together in a crèche. Breed throughout year, but there is a birth-peak.

Longevity 17 years in captivity.

Calls Distinctive whistles by territorial rams, also indicating alarm.

Occurrence Ruaha (Tanzania). Over 40 000 in Tanzania; do not occur elsewhere in region. Reduced in range and numbers.

MEASUREMENTS
Weight: ♂ 74 kg; ♀ 62 kg
Shoulder height: 80 cm
Total length: 1.5–1.7 m
Tail length: 28 cm
Record horn length (EA): 54.61 cm
  (Kilombero, Tanzania)

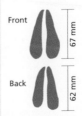

Front — 67 mm

Back — 62 mm

BOHOR REEDBUCK

Redunca redunca

Swahili: *Tohe, Forhi* **German:** *Gemeiner Riedbock* **French:** *Redunca*

Identification pointers Small to medium-sized antelope with no outstanding features. Overall body colour yellowish to pale red-brown, and underparts white. Tail short, bushy and brown above, white below. Bare, grey patch below each ear. Only ram carries short, stout, ringed, forward-hooked horns.

Similar See mountain reedbuck, but separated by habitat; little range overlap with larger common reedbuck. Kob in western Uganda has different horn form and distinctive white markings.

Habitat Tied to river floodplains, reed beds and seasonally flooded grassland.

Behaviour Territorial rams may have up to 5 ewes and their lambs in their ranges, but sometimes larger numbers gather temporarily at the site of a sought-after food source. In a study undertaken in Serengeti, male territories ranged between 25 and 60 ha in size. Ewes, rather than territory, are defended. In areas of prime habitat, groups may reach densities of 110 animals to the km² (as recorded in north-east Uganda). Bachelor groups generally tolerated by territory-holding rams, but chased off when ewes are in vicinity. Most feeding apparently takes place at night.

Food Grasses.

Reproduction Through much of its range there is no distinct birth season, although peaks suspected in some areas. Single fawn dropped after about 210–220-days' gestation.

Longevity 10 years in captivity.

Calls Nasal whistles.

Occurrence Serengeti, Ngorongoro, Tarangire, Mikumi, Ruaha, Katavi (Tanzania); Masai Mara, Lake Nakuru (Kenya); Queen Elizabeth, Murchison Falls, Kidepo (Uganda). An estimated 100 000 occur in region, but populations increasingly fragmented.

MEASUREMENTS
Weight: ♂ 45–65 kg; ♀ 35–55 kg
Shoulder height: ♂ 70–90 cm; ♀ 65–80 cm
Total length: ♂ 1.4–1.7 m; ♀ 1.3–1.5 m
Tail length: ♂ 20–25 cm; ♀ 15–23 cm
Record horn length (EA): 37.47 cm (Tanzania)

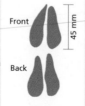

Front

Back

45 mm

COMMON REEDBUCK

Redunca arundinum

Swahili: *Tohe ya kusini* **German:** *Großer Riedbock* **French:** *Cobe des roseaux*

Identification pointers Medium-sized antelope; the largest of the 3 reedbuck species occurring in the region. Uniform brown or greyish-fawn upperparts; head and neck usually slightly paler, but underparts and underside of tail white. Usually has pale to white patch on upper throat. Vertical black stripe on the forward-facing surface of the front legs. Only the ram carries fairly long, forward-curved horns, strongly ringed from the base for about two-thirds of their length. Base of horns usually narrowly ringed with pale grey growth tissue.

Similar See bohor reedbuck; range in region does not overlap with mountain reedbuck. See puku in southern Tanzania.

Habitat Occupies areas with tall grass and reed beds, close to permanent water.

Behaviour Does not form herds, but lives in pairs or small family parties. In areas of prime habitat, larger numbers may be seen feeding in close proximity. Territories defended by rams. Most activity takes place at night, but in undisturbed areas may be seen feeding in cooler daylight hours.

Food Mainly grasses, but will also browse occasionally.

Reproduction Young born at any time of year, and single fawn, weighing approximately 4.5 kg, dropped after a 220-day gestation. Fawn remains hidden for about first 2 months of life. After each suckling session (once or twice daily), fawn moves to new lying-up location.

Longevity 10 years in captivity.

Calls Sharp, nasal whistle common.

Occurrence Ruaha, Selous (Tanzania). Only in Tanzania and mainly in south.

MEASUREMENTS
Weight: ♂ 43–68 kg; ♀ 32–51 kg
Shoulder height: ♂ 95 cm; ♀ 80 cm
Total length: ♂ 1.6–1.8 m;
♀ 1.4–1.7 m
Tail length: 25 cm
Record horn length (EA): 40.01 cm
(Tabora, Tanzania)

Front

65 mm

Back

61 mm

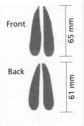

MOUNTAIN REEDBUCK

Redunca fulvorufula

Swahili: *Tohe ya milima* **German:** *Bergriedbock* **French:** *Redunca de montagne*

Identification pointers Smallest of reedbuck species, with grey-fawn to reddish-brown upperparts and white underparts, including area below bushy tail. Hair on neck and head usually more yellow-fawn, and lower legs often paler than rest of upper body. Ears long and narrow, lined with white hairs on inner surface. Only ram carries short, stout, forward-curved and heavily ringed horns. Bare glandular patch below each ear.

Similar Can be separated from common and bohor reedbuck on habitat; also both species larger.

Habitat Mountainous and rocky slopes, but showing preference for broken hill country with scattered trees, bush clumps and open grassy slopes. Recorded as high as 5 000 m on Mt Kilimanjaro.

Behaviour Rams attempt to hold territory on year-round basis, but small groups of 2–6 ewes and their young are less stable and move from herd to herd. These groups cross freely through territories of rams, but may spend long periods within the range of a single ram. Small bachelor herds also form, but these are unstable. May feed at night or during the day. Can be very difficult to spot when standing still on grassed hillslope.

Food Predominantly grasses.

Reproduction Young may be born at any time of year, but birth-peaks evident in some areas during rains. Single lamb, weighing about 3 kg, born after gestation of some 242 days. The lamb remains hidden for first 2–3 months.

Longevity 12 years.

Calls Usually only alarm and territorial nasal whistles heard.

Occurrence Mt Kilimanjaro, Ngorongoro (Tanzania); Meru, Lake Nakuru, Nairobi, Chyulu Hills, Tsavo (Kenya).Very fragmented in East Africa and threatened outside conservation areas.

MEASUREMENTS
Weight: 30 kg
Shoulder height: 72 cm
Total length: 1.3–1.5 m
Tail length: 20 cm
Record horn length (EA):
  23.50 cm (Momella, Tanzania)

Front

43 mm

Back

45 mm

COKE'S HARTEBEEST/KONGONI   *Alcelaphus buselaphus cokei*

Swahili: *Kongoni* **German:** *Kongoni* **French:** *Bubale de Coke*

Identification pointers Medium-sized; shoulders higher than rump, which gives it an awkward appearance. Among fastest of antelope. Head long and pointed, as are the narrow ears. Tail very short-haired at base and over much of under surface, but with longish dark brown to black hairs on outer surface. Overall coat colour is reddish-brown to sandy-fawn, with area of rump and underparts paler. Both sexes carry widely spread u-shaped horns, with tips moderately back-pointed and clearly ringed.

Similar In Uganda small populations of Lelwel's hartebeest (*A. b. lelwel*) occur; very similar appearance; horns differ slightly. See much darker-coloured topi with black facial blaze and different horn structure.

Habitat Open savanna country and lightly wooded grassland, extending into more arid country after rain.

Behaviour Usually herds of about 20; gatherings of hundreds not uncommon. Large groups normally associated with onset of rains. Adult bulls territorial; harem herds stay temporarily within such a male's territory, which generally contains prime grazing. Bachelor herds occupy areas around these territories; usually poorer grazing. Active by day, but will feed at night.

Food Mainly grasses, but sometimes low shrubs and herbaceous plants.

Reproduction Single calf, born after about 240-day gestation, usually just before, or at onset of, the rains.

Longevity 19 years in captivity.

Calls Frog-like quacks and grunts.

Occurrence Serengeti, Ngorongoro, Tarangire (Tanzania); Tsavo, Masai Mara, Nairobi, Hell's Gate (Kenya). Substantial numbers in several conservation areas still; has declined elsewhere.

MEASUREMENTS
Weight: ♂ 150 kg; ♀ 120 kg
Shoulder height: 1.25 m
Total length: 2.3 m
Tail length: 47 cm
Record horn length (EA):
60.96 cm (Kenya)

Front

100 mm

■ *A. b. cokei*
■ *A. b. lelwel*

LICHTENSTEIN'S HARTEBEEST

Alcelaphus lichtensteinii

Swahili: *Kongoni* **German:** *Lichtenstein-Kuhantilope, Lichtenstein-Antilope* **French:** *Bubale de Lichtenstein*

Identification pointers Has typical hartebeest form, with shoulders higher than rump. Tail is short-haired at base and over much of under surface, but with longish dark brown to black hairs on outer surface. Has long, slender head with narrow, pointed ears. Overall body colour is yellow-fawn to pale reddish-fawn, with slightly darker saddle stretching from shoulders to rump. Flanks, rump and lower legs are paler in colour, and the rump is often off-white. Both sexes carry horns that are flattened at the base, strongly ringed (except at tips), and with z-shaped curvature.

Similar Can only be confused with Coke's hartebeest (*kongoni*), but ranges do not overlap.

Habitat Savanna woodland adjoining marshy areas and floodplains, with access to drinking water.

Behaviour Normally in small nursery herds of up to 10 individuals; larger, temporary herds may occur. Territorial bull stays with group of cows and their young within fixed home range, which usually incorporates best grazing. Bachelor herds utilise less favourable grazing grounds. Hierarchy exists among females, with older cows dominant. Mainly feed by day, but nocturnal grazing not unusual.

Food Almost exclusively grass-eaters.

Reproduction Single calf, weighing about 15 kg, dropped after 240-day gestation. Calf may follow mother soon after birth, but lies out in the open between suckling sessions.

Longevity No age known, but probably similar to Coke's hartebeest.

Calls Frog-like quacks and grunts. Not particularly vocal.

Occurrence Selous, Ruaha, Katavi, Mikumi (Tanzania). Probably >50 000 animals in Tanzania (in region, the only country in which they occur).

MEASUREMENTS
Weight: ♂ 170 kg; ♀ 165 kg
Shoulder height: 1.25 m
Total length: 2.01–2.5 m
Tail length: 48 cm
Record horn length (EA):
  61.28 cm (Tanzania)

Front

100 mm

TOPI

Damaliscus lunatus jimela

Swahili: *Nyamera* **German:** *Jimela* **French:** *Topi*

Identification pointers Hartebeest-like in overall appearance, with shoulders higher than rump. Face elongated and narrow, with dark frontal blaze. Upperparts dark reddish-brown, with head, lower shoulders and upper hind legs usually darker in colour. Lower parts of legs brownish-yellow, as is inner rump region. Tail has distinctive dark tassel towards the tip. Horns present in both sexes, prominently ringed except at the tip, and narrowly lyrate in form.

Similar Coke's hartebeest and Lichtenstein's hartebeest much lighter in colour and with different horn forms.

Habitat Open savanna woodland adjoining grassland plains.

Behaviour Usually form nursery herds of 15–30 animals, but larger groups not unusual. During rutting season adult bulls establish territories across which nursery herds move freely. Bulls attempt to keep cows that are receptive within their territories, for mating. These territories may be held as mating grounds for short periods, while larger areas are held by resident female herds. Outside the rut, bulls circulate freely. Topi often mix with other plains game.

Food Show preference for short to medium-length grasses, and especially new growth.

Reproduction Single calf, weighing 10–12 kg, born after about 240-day gestation; able to keep up with the herd a short time after birth. Birth seasons linked closely to onset of rainy seasons.

Longevity 9 years in wild; 12–15 years in captivity.

Calls Frog-like quacks and grunts.

Occurrence Akagera (Rwanda); Queen Elizabeth (Uganda); Serengeti, Ngorongoro (Tanzania); Masai Mara (Kenya). They still occur in substantial numbers, but mainly within conservation areas.

MEASUREMENTS
Weight: ♂ 140 kg; ♀ 125 kg
Shoulder height: 1.2 m
Total length: 2.1 m
Tail length: 45 cm
Record horn length (EA):
 61.91 cm (Bugungu, Uganda)

Front

90 mm

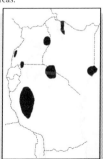

BLUE WILDEBEEST

Connochaetes taurinus

Swahili: *Nyumbu ya montu* **German:** *Streifengnu, Weißbartgnu, Njassa-Gnu* **French:** *Gnou à queue noire*

Identification pointers Lightly built hindquarters, but more robust at shoulders and chest. Head large, with broad snout. Both sexes carry horns that grow outwards, turn sharply up and then turn inwards; horn bases form a separated boss. Black, horse-like tail. Overall coat colour dark grey, tinged with brown and with a number of vertical, darker stripes on neck and chest. In northern, white-bearded races (*C. t. mearnsi* and *C. t. albojubatus*) long throat fringe is dirty white; in Selous, the *C. t johnstoni* race has a distinct white chevron across the muzzle and a dark throat fringe.

Similar African buffalo much larger, with heavier horns and no throat fringe.

Habitat Open grassland savanna and savanna woodland.

Behaviour Live in herds numbering up to 30 individuals, but form vast congregations while still maintaining herd integrity (such as in Serengeti).

Some populations resident, but others highly nomadic, following the rains and new plant growth. Territorial bulls defend zone around their cows, even when migrating. While a territorial bull may control 2–150 cows, latter may wander through mobile territories of several bulls.

Food Prefer short green grass if available.

Reproduction In Serengeti/ Ngorongoro ecosystem, calves born February and March. Single calf, about 22 kg, dropped after 250-day gestation.

Longevity 18 years in wild; 20 captive.

Calls Characteristic metallic *gnou* grunts; calls of bulls in migratory herds have been likened to chorus of immense frogs.

Occurrence Selous, Tarangire, Serengeti, Ngorongoro (Tanzania); Masai Mara, Amboseli, Nairobi (Kenya). In Serengeti/ Masai Mara ecosystem, up to 1.5 million; substantial numbers in Selous ecosystem. Major declines outside protected areas.

MEASUREMENTS
Weight: ♂ 250 kg; ♀ 180 kg
Shoulder height: ♂ 1.5 m; ♀ 1.3 m
Total length: 2.4–3.3 m
Tail length: 45 cm–1 m
Record horn length (EA):
Johnston's 84.14 cm;
white-bearded 81.28 cm

Front

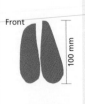

100 mm

C. t. johnstoni
C. t. albojubatus and
C. t. mearnsi

♂ ♀

IMPALA

Aepyceros melampus

Swahili: *Swala pala* **German:** *Impala* **French:** *Impala*

Identification pointers Medium-sized antelope, lightly built and graceful, with reddish-fawn upperparts becoming paler on sides. White chest, belly, throat and chin. Tail is white with central black line on upper surface and each buttock has vertical black blaze. Only antelope with tuft of black hair on lower rear-edge of back leg. Rams carry long, graceful lyrate horns that are deeply ringed for most of their length.

Similar Nothing really similar, but see bohor reedbuck and common reedbuck (coloration and horns differ). Also see gerenuk and Grant's gazelle.

Habitat Open or light savanna woodland, avoiding open grassland unless adjoining bush cover. Access to drinking water essential.

Behaviour Nursery herds of ewes and young may overlap with seasonal territories of several rams. During breeding season – tied closely to onset of the rains – territorial rams separate out 15–20 ewes for mating. Bachelor herds tend to occupy areas away from breeding herds. Active mainly during cooler daylight hours, but also feed at night. Outside the rut, rams live in bachelor herds.

Food True mixed feeders: both grasses and browse eaten, with quantities varying between areas and seasons.

Reproduction Single lamb, about 5 kg, dropped after about 196-day gestation. Lambs group together in crèches.

Longevity 12 years; 15 in captivity.

Calls Rams very vocal during the rut, with repertoire of growls, roars and snorts. Roars can be heard for up to 2 km.

Occurrence Ruaha, Lake Manyara, Ngorongoro, Serengeti, Mikumi, Selous (Tanzania); Samburu, Meru, Nairobi, Tsavo (Kenya). Still common and widespread; can be found in many conservation areas.

MEASUREMENTS
Weight: ♂ 50 kg; ♀ 40 kg
Shoulder height: 90 cm
Total length: 1.6–1.72 m
Tail length: 28 cm
Record horn length (EA): 91.76 cm
  (South Masai Reserve, Kenya)

Front

47 mm

GERENUK

Litocranius walleri

Swahili: *Swala twiga* **German:** *Gerenuk, Giraffengazelle* **French:** *Gazelle de Waller*

Identification pointers Easy to identify because of very long legs and long, thin neck, and for this reason alternative English name is 'giraffe-necked antelope'. Upperparts rufous-fawn in colour, with paler sides. A thin, dark line separates white underparts. Head short, with somewhat pinched appearance. Eyes very large, and ringed with white. Ears long and pointed. Only rams carry characteristic horns, which are relatively short, robust, heavily ringed and resemble a tight lyre shape.

Similar Impala and Grant's gazelle have shorter legs and neck, as well as different horn structure.

Habitat Arid thorn scrub and thicket.

Behaviour Mainly solitary, but small mixed groups with single ram common, as are groups of ewes and lambs. Rarely >8 animals seen together, and usually spaced several metres apart when feeding or lying up. When feeding, long legs and neck are distinct advantage, increasing reach. Also able to stand erect on hind legs when browsing. Home range of single animal covers 2–6 km². Rams highly territorial and drive away any intruding rams. Resident in specific areas and not migratory.

Food Strict browsers, selecting new leaf growth, buds, fresh twig tips and flowers of a range of tree and bush species, but strongly favouring acacia species. Independent of water.

Reproduction Single lamb, weighing about 3 kg, born after 210-day gestation. Births coincide with the rains.

Longevity 10–12 years in wild, but less in captivity.

Calls Normally silent.

Occurrence Tsavo, Samburu, Meru (Kenya). Total population about 80 000, majority of which in East Africa. Most important populations in Kenya.

MEASUREMENTS
Weight: 30–50 kg
Shoulder height: 95 cm–1 m
Total length: 1.8–1.95 m
Tail length: 25–35 cm
Record horn length (EA):
44.77 cm (Isiolo, Kenya)

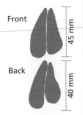

Front

45 mm

Back

40 mm

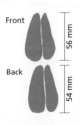

SOEMMERING'S GAZELLE

Gazella soemmeringi

Swahili: *Aoul* **German:** *Sömmering-Gazelle* **French:** *Gazelle de Soemmering*

Identification pointers Relatively large gazelle, with distinctly white rump and upper surface of tail; underparts also white. Indistinct, slightly darker flank stripe present in some individuals. Distinctive black and white facial markings. Rest of body and outer leg surfaces pale rufous-fawn. Both sexes carry rather long, ringed horns. Ewe's horns more slender, similar to those of Grant's gazelle, but shorter and more inward-pointing.

Similar See Grant's gazelle in far northern Kenya, as well as gerenuk, but latter has proportionally longer legs and neck.

Habitat Semi-arid grassland, open scrub and hilly country, usually dominated by acacia trees and bushes.

Behaviour Live in small herds that usually consist of family parties, but larger herds form temporarily. In some parts of range, movements dictated chiefly by sporadic rainfall that encourages new vegetation growth. Dynamics of these movements poorly understood. Larger herds include rams and ewes, but adult rams frequently solitary. Herds commonly associate with other antelope species. This gazelle has not been studied in detail.

Food Mixed feeders, taking grass and browse.

Reproduction Single lamb, weighing up to 4.5 kg, dropped after gestation of about 198 days. Strongly seasonal, with lambs dropped in April and May.

Longevity 14 years on record.

Calls Subdued grunts.

Occurrence Not present in any protected areas. Populations greatly reduced by uncontrolled hunting across its range, but still occur in reasonable numbers. In Kenya known only in area that adjoins Ethiopia in north-east.

MEASUREMENTS
Weight: 35–45 kg
Shoulder height: 85–90 cm
Total length: 1.4–1.78 m
Tail length: 18–28 cm
Record horn length (EA):
  52.07 cm (Ethiopia)

Front

56 mm

Back

54 mm

♂

♀

GRANT'S GAZELLE

Gazella granti

Swahili: *Swala granti* **German:** *Grant-Gazelle* **French:** *Gazelle de Grant*

Identification pointers Largest gazelle in East Africa; uniformly fawn upperparts and white underparts, including inner leg surfaces. Distinct vertical black stripe on either side of white buttocks. Lateral body stripe usually very faint. Circle of white hair surrounds eye and extends as white stripe to snout. Magnificent horns carried by both sexes; those of ram more robust. Horns long, well-ringed and slope slightly backwards and then outwards, with points turning inwards. Several races recognised on basis of horn forms, those of *G. g. robertsi* being more widely spread, and having downward pointing tips.

Similar Soemmering's gazelle in northern Kenya, with different horns and facial markings. Thomson's gazelle much smaller, with prominent lateral stripe and all-black tail.

Habitat From semi-desert scrub to open savanna woodland.

Behaviour Usually small herds of up to 30 ewes and their offspring, with 1 adult ram. Adult territorial rams execute elaborate displays when confronting each other. Young and non-territorial rams form bachelor groups that move around edges of territorial ram ranges. In some areas, herds have fixed home ranges, in others they are seasonally nomadic and temporarily form larger herds. Mingle freely with other ungulates.

Food Mixed; take grasses and browse.

Reproduction Young born any time of year, but in arid areas most births tied to the rains. Single fawn, weighing 5–7 kg, born after about 198-day gestation.

Longevity 12 years; less in captivity.

Calls Snorts.

Occurrence Ngorongoro, Serengeti, Ruaha (Tanzania); Samburu, Lake Turkana, Meru, Nairobi, Masai Mara, Amboseli, Tsavo (Kenya); Kidepo (Uganda). Probably >300 000, most in East Africa.

MEASUREMENTS
Weight: ♂ 55–80 kg; ♀ 35–50 kg
Shoulder height: ♂ 85–95 cm; ♀ 80–85 cm
Total length: ♂ 1.5–1.8 cm; ♀ 1.2–1.4 m
Tail length: ♂ 25–35 cm; ♀ 25–30 cm
Record horn length (EA): 80.65 cm (N. Kimali, Tanzania)

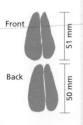

Front

Back

51 mm

50 mm

THOMSON'S GAZELLE

Gazella thomsoni

Swahili: *Swala tomi, Lala* **German:** *Thomson-Gazelle* **French:** *Gazelle de Thomson*

Identification pointers Small gazelle, with pale yellowish-fawn to reddish-fawn upperparts. Distinct dark band separates upperparts from bright white underparts. Has white ring around eye. Short, constantly flicking tail covered with black hair. Horns grow close together and are strongly ringed – those of ram fairly long; those of ewe short, slender and often deformed. In East Africa often called 'Tommy'.

Similar Grant's gazelle much larger, lacks dark lateral line and has white and black tail.

Habitat Open savanna grassland.

Behaviour Form small herds of up to 60 animals, led by an old female and accompanied by a single mature male. Herds not stable, and individuals constantly leave and join. Rams most territorial during rut, but at other times this is largely not in evidence and thousands may gather and mingle on feeding grounds. Territories very small, averaging 100–300 m in diameter. In the rut, rams fight aggressively for territorial rights and there is very little ritual or posturing involved. When threatened, both sexes pronk (make stiff-legged jumps) with white rump hairs flared.

Food Mainly grazers.

Reproduction Lambs seen at any time of year, but most dropped towards end of rainy season. Single lamb, weighing 2–3 kg, born after gestation of about 188 days.

Longevity >10 years on record.

Calls Grunts and snorts.

Occurrence Serengeti, Ngorongoro (Tanzania); Masai Mara, Amboseli, Nairobi, Lake Nakuru (Kenya). >500 000 occur, mainly in conservation areas. Increased greatly in Serengeti as growing wildebeest population has given them access to cropped grass.

MEASUREMENTS
Weight: 15–25 kg
Shoulder height: 55–65 cm
Total length: 1–1.38 m
Tail length: 20–28 cm
Record horn length (EA):
  43.82 cm (location unknown)

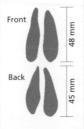

Front

48 mm

Back

45 mm

SUNI

Neotragus moschatus

Swahili: *Paa, Suni* **German:** *Moschusböckchen* **French:** *Suni*

Identification pointers Tiny, elegant dwarf antelope, with rich rufous-brown upperparts flecked with white hairs. Underparts white to off-white. Has 2 slightly curved white bars on throat, and above each hoof a narrow, dark band. Tail is dark brown above, has white tip and is flicked regularly and rapidly. Only ram carries short, thick, prominently ridged horns that slope backwards in line with the face. Rather transparent, pink-lined ears.

Similar See bigger Sharpe's grysbok, which has much more white flecking on coat and very short tail; also dik-diks, with crest on forehead, elongated snout and tiny tail.

Habitat Dry thickets and riverine woodland with dense undergrowth.

Behaviour Usually occur in pairs or small groups of 1 adult ram and up to 4 ewes with associated young. Rams are territorial, marking areas with glandular deposits and dung heaps. Active mainly at night but also during cooler hours of daylight. When disturbed, run off in zig-zag pattern, similar to that of startled hare. Use regular pathways, making them very vulnerable to snaring.

Food Browse of most importance, but they feed on wide range of plant species.

Reproduction Young born at any time of year, but birth-peaks in some areas. In northern Tanzania, birth-peak between November and February. Single fawn dropped after about 180-day gestation. Fawn remains hidden for first few weeks of life, only emerging to suckle.

Longevity 9 years on record.

Calls Wheezing screech when alarmed.

Occurrence Still common over much of its range, including on Unguja (Zanzibar); Arusha, Mt Kilimanjaro, Selous (Tanzania); Mt Kenya, Aberdares, Amboseli (Kenya).

MEASUREMENTS
Weight: 5 kg
Shoulder height: 35 cm
Total length: 68–75 cm
Tail length: 12 cm
Record horn length (EA): 10.16 cm (Mt Kenya)

Front

23 mm

Back

22 mm

ORIBI

Ourebia ourebi

Swahili: *Taya* **German:** *Oribi, Bleichböckchen* **French:** *Ourébi*

Identification pointers Largest of the dwarf antelope, with rufous yellow-orange upperparts and white underparts and inner thighs. Neck relatively long and slender, ears medium-sized and short tail has prominent black tip. Hair on back often has curly appearance. Only the ram carries short, erect and partly ridged horns. Marking gland visible below ear.

Similar Steenbok smaller, smooth-coated, with very short reddish-brown tail and large ears; little range overlap.

Habitat Open, short grassland with taller grass patches to provide cover.

Behaviour Occur in pairs or small parties with 1 adult ram and up to 4 ewes. Ram is vigorously territorial and marks grass stalks with facial gland secretions; droppings deposited in communal dung heaps. Animals very bound to range and rarely leave, even when under stress. When disturbed, run rapidly, with occasional pronks (stiff-legged jumps),

clearly displaying black-tipped tail; after covering a short distance, they usually stop and turn towards threat.

Food Principally grazers, but browse taken on occasion. Show marked preference for short grass; will move to another part of range if grass gets too long.

Reproduction Births occur throughout the year, with distinct peaks during the rains. Single lamb born after about 210-day gestation, remaining hidden for first 3–4 months of life.

Longevity 14 years in captivity.

Calls Sharp whistle or sneeze when alarmed.

Occurrence Akagera (Rwanda); Kidepo, Murchison Falls, Queen Elizabeth, Lake Mburo (Uganda); Selous, Katavi, Ngorongoro, Serengeti, Tarangire (Tanzania); Masai Mara, Tsavo (Kenya). Very patchy, but widespread in region; wiped out by hunting and habitat loss in some areas.

MEASUREMENTS
Weight: 14–20 kg (♂ averages 2 kg lighter than ♀)
Shoulder height: 60 cm
Total length: 1.1 m
Tail length: 6–15 cm
Record horn length (EA): 17.78 cm (Debasian Mts)

Front
40 mm

Back
42 mm

STEENBOK

Raphicerus campestris

Swahili: *Tondoro, Funo, Isha* **German:** *Steinböckchen* **French:** *Steenbok*

Identification pointers Small, elegant dwarf antelope with large eyes and very large ears. Upperparts normally rufous-fawn to deeper chestnut colour. White underparts. Pale fawn to white patch usually present on throat, as well as white above eyes. Very short tail a uniform rufous-fawn. Only the ram carries short, sharp-pointed, smooth-surfaced horns that rise near-vertically from head.

Similar See oribi, which is larger, with black-tipped tail and smaller ears.

Habitat Open country with some cover and will penetrate arid areas along dry riverbeds. Independent of drinking water.

Behaviour Solitary or in ram/ewe pairs, with both sexes being strongly defensive of their joint territories. Unlike other antelope, they defecate and urinate in shallow scrapes dug with front hoofs, and then cover them. Lie up in cover during heat of day, feeding during cooler hours. Nocturnal feeding also common, especially in areas where they are regularly hunted or disturbed. In suitable habitat they can reach quite high densities.

Food Mixed feeders that take grasses, browse, seed pods and fruits. During dry periods they dig out roots and bulbs with front hoofs.

Reproduction Single lamb, weighing approximately 900 g, dropped after gestation of some 170 days. Lambs remain hidden for first few weeks after birth. Young born in the region throughout year.

Longevity 10–12 years.

Calls Alarm snorts.

Occurrence Ngorongoro, Serengeti, Ruaha (Tanzania); Tsavo, Amboseli, Masai Mara, Nairobi (Kenya). Fairly widespread in region, but has disappeared from number of areas and range now reduced.

MEASUREMENTS
Weight: 11 kg
Shoulder height: 50 cm
Total length: 75–90 cm
Tail length: 5 cm
Record horn length (EA):
  15.24 cm (Rift Valley, Kenya)

Front

Back

40 mm

40 mm

SHARPE'S GRYSBOK

Raphicerus sharpei

Swahili: *Dondoro* **German:** *Sharpe-Greisbock* **French:** *Grysbok de Sharpe*

Identification pointers Small and stockily built. Reddish-brown upperparts, liberally flecked with white hairs, giving grizzled appearance. Underparts buff to buffy-white but never pure white. Fairly short in the leg. Only the ram carries short, sharp-pointed, smooth, slightly back-angled horns. Tail very short and the same colour as upper body.

Similar Suni much smaller, not as strongly grizzled and with longish black and white tail; ram's horns strongly ringed.

Habitat Requires areas with good vegetation cover, especially low thicket with adjacent open grassed patches. Commonly associated with vegetated rocky hills and in scrub at their base. In region, occur only in Tanzania, where restricted mainly to areas of *Brachystegia* woodland.

Behaviour Although mainly nocturnal, quite often seen during cooler daylight hours and on overcast days. Normally solitary, but usually a pair lives in loose association within same home range. Rams believed to be territorial, but have been little studied. Territories are marked with large dung middens, and secretions from the gland in front of the eye are rubbed onto twigs and plant stalks.

Food Mostly browse, taking leaves, pods, fruits and berries, but also eat some grass and will dig for roots and bulbs with front hoofs.

Reproduction Lambs may be dropped at any time of year, and births may peak with the rains. Single lamb born after 200-day gestation.

Longevity Not known, but probably at least 10 years.

Calls Quiet bleat, rarely heard.

Occurrence Selous (Tanzania). Not uncommon, but are secretive and seldom seen.

MEASUREMENTS
Weight: 7.5 kg
Shoulder height: 50 cm
Total length: 65–80 cm
Tail length: 6 cm
Record horn length: 10.48 cm

Front

34 mm

KLIPSPRINGER

Oreotragus oreotragus

Swahili: *Mbuzi mawe, Ngurunguru* **German:** *Klippspringer* **French:** *Oréotrague*

Identification pointers Small and stocky, with very short tail, coarse, spiny hair usually yellow-brown to grey-brown, and overall grizzled appearance. Paler underparts; generally grey-white to brownish-white. Ears rounded, broad and typically bordered with black, but inner hairs white. Rams carry short horns, widely separated at base, vertical and only ringed close to the head. In some populations (parts of Tanzania and north-east Uganda) fairly high percentage of females have horns. Walk on tips of hoofs.

Similar Habitat should separate it from any other species in region, but see Sharpe's grysbok.

Habitat Rugged, rocky areas from coastal hills to 4 500 m above sea level (on Mt Meru).

Behaviour Live in pairs or small family parties. The ram is strongly territorial. Communal dung middens scattered through home range, and both sexes mark twigs with secretions from glands in front of the eyes. Choice of home range dependent on food quality and abundance, varying in size from 8–49 ha. Extremely agile even in very rugged, rocky terrain. Most active during cooler daylight hours, or throughout the day when overcast or cool.

Food Predominantly browsers, but eat green grass when available.

Reproduction May be seasonal birth-peaks in some areas, but lambs usually dropped in any month of year. Single lamb, about 1 kg, after about 210-day gestation; hidden for first 1–3 months.

Longevity 15 years in captivity.

Calls Loud nasal whistle, snorts.

Occurrence Selous, Ruaha, Ngorongoro, Serengeti, Lake Manyara, Mt Kilimanjaro, Mt Meru, near Arusha (Tanzania); Samburu, Tsavo, Lake Bogoria, Mt Kenya (Kenya); Kidepo (Uganda). Still fairly common in East Africa.

MEASUREMENTS
Weight: ♂ 10 kg; ♀ 13 kg
Shoulder height: 50–60 cm
Total length: 80 cm–1 m
Tail length: 8 cm
Record horn length (EA):
  13.34 cm (Mount Kenya)

Front

20 mm

KIRK'S DIK-DIK

Madoqua kirki

Swahili: *Digidigi, Suguya* **German:** *Kirk-Dikdik* **French:** *Dik-dik de Kirk*

Identification pointers Elongated, very mobile snout (not as well developed as Guenther's dik-dik). Very small, delicate antelope, with upperparts yellowish-grey and grizzled. Neck paler than shoulders and flanks, and underparts white to creamish in colour; lower legs fawnish-yellow. White ring of short hairs circles the eye. Only rams have short, spiky, ringed horns. Has distinctive crest of erectile hairs on forehead.

Similar Although very different, see Sharpe's grysbok and suni.

Habitat Relatively arid bush country, favouring areas with acacia trees or bushes, as long as dense undergrowth is available. Also occupy bush-covered hillslopes and fringing scrub cover.

Behaviour Usually live singly, in pairs or in small family parties. Pairs live within defended territory and mate for life. Pairs establish communal dung middens within home range, and twigs are marked with secretions from scent glands in front of their large eyes. Active during day and night. Within territories, regularly used pathways radiate from resting and feeding sites. Head crest raised during territorial conflict and other social interactions.

Food Browse most important; also eat green grass. Will dig for roots and bulbs with front hoofs, especially in dry season.

Reproduction Single fawn, 600–760 g, dropped after some 170 days. Birth-peaks seem linked to the rains.

Longevity 4 years in wild; 10 years in captivity.

Calls Nasal whistling alarm and contact calls, also used to establish territory; *zik-zik* alarm; bleats and squeals when under stress.

Occurrence Ruaha, Ngorongoro, Serengeti (Tanzania); Tsavo, Masai Mara, Samburu, Meru (Kenya). Still quite common throughout region.

MEASUREMENTS
Weight: 5 kg
Shoulder height: 38 cm
Total length: 64–76 cm
Tail length: 4 cm
Record horn length (EA):
  11.43 cm (Ikoma, Tanzania)

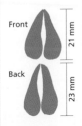

Front

21 mm

Back

23 mm

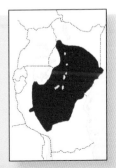

GUENTHER'S DIK-DIK

Madoqua guentheri

Swahili: *Digidigi, Suguya* **German:** *Günther-Dikdik* **French:** *Dik-dik de Günther*

Identification pointers Has the most elongated and proboscis-like snout of all dik-dik species. Overall body colour greyish-fawn, with distinct grizzling; underparts white. Lower legs may be reddish-fawn, but without grizzled appearance. Head usually more reddish than upperparts. White ring around eye often absent or less conspicuous than in Kirk's dik-dik.

Similar See Kirk's dik-dik where range overlaps in northern Kenya and north-east Uganda. Salt's dik-dik (*M. saltiana*) occurs in extreme north-eastern Kenya, has grey speckled back, with legs, forehead and snout bright red-brown.

Habitat Similar to Kirk's dik-dik where ranges overlap, but extend into more arid country across northern Kenya. Require areas with low thicket vegetation, but drinking water not required.

Behaviour Similar in most respects to Kirk's dik-dik, being territorial and marking range with dung middens and secretions from gland in front of the eye. Before defecating and urinating on midden, will first scratch at earlier deposits with front hoofs. Evidence exists that pairs live within defended territories and mate for life.

Food Mainly browsers, taking leaves, pods, flowers and fruits, but will take green grass when available; also dig for roots, bulbs and corms.

Reproduction Single young, 600–760 g, born after about 172-day gestation. Ram and ewe care for young.

Longevity 4–5 years in wild.

Calls Nasal whistles of different intensity; *zik-zik* alarm call and hiss.

Occurrence Kidepo (Uganda); Samburu, Lake Turkana, Marsabit, Lake Bogoria, Tsavo (Kenya). Most abundant dik-dik in Kenya and, although hunted, this probably has little impact on population size.

MEASUREMENTS
Weight: 3.7–5.5 kg
Shoulder height: 34–38 cm
Total length: 62–70 cm
Tail length: 3–5 cm
Record horn length (EA):
  10.80 cm

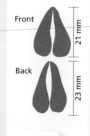

Front

21 mm

Back

23 mm

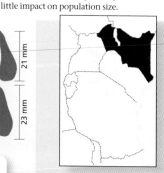

COMMON (GREY) DUIKER
Sylvicapra grimmia

Swahili: *Nsya* **German:** *Kronenducker* **French:** *Céphalophe de Grimm*

Identification pointers Fairly small antelope; usually has distinctive crest of longish hair on top of the head and a black facial blaze. Variable coloration has been used to name many races; however, all are this single species. Most coloration falls within light grey to reddish-brown to dark brown, with underparts marginally paler to white. Front surfaces of legs usually darker. The only duiker that has a straight back when standing or walking. Only the ram carries the well-ringed, sharp-pointed horns.

Similar See other duikers, but they walk with arched backs, and few share the same habitat; see smaller Sharpe's grysbok, with grizzled red-brown coat and different horn form.

Habitat Very wide habitat tolerance, but mainly occupy savanna woodland, thickets and open bush country.

Behaviour Normally solitary, but pairs commonly seen. In areas of high density several individuals may feed in close proximity. Rams hold and mark territories, within which there is usually 1 ewe. Ram drives away other rams; female chases away other ewes. Most active at night, but frequently feed during cooler daylight hours.

Food Very wide range of plants, especially browse; seek out and eat animal food such as termites, locusts, even birds.

Reproduction Single lamb, about 1.6 kg, after a gestation of about 190 days. Born at any time; some areas show birth-peaks coinciding with the rains.

Longevity 12 years in captivity.

Calls Normally silent, but alarm bleats and soft snorts.

Occurrence Kidepo, Murchison Falls, Queen Elizabeth, Lake Mburo (Uganda); Tsavo, Shimba Hills, Amboseli, Masai Mara, Nairobi, Marsabit, Aberdares, Mt Kenya (Kenya); nearly all parks in Tanzania. Abundant and widespread.

MEASUREMENTS
Weight: ♂ 18 kg; ♀ 21 kg
Shoulder height: 50 cm
Total length: 90–135 cm
Tail length: 10–22 cm
Record horn length (EA):
   15.56 cm (Tanzania)

Front

38 mm

YELLOW-BACKED DUIKER
Cephalophus silvicultor

Swahili: *Kipoke* **German:** *Gelbrückenducker* **French:** *Céphalophe à dos jaune*

Identification pointers By far the largest duiker in East Africa and easily identified by its overall dark brown to blackish coat and distinctive yellow rump patch, which is broadest above the tail and narrows to a point just behind the shoulders. These yellow hairs are erectile and are raised when the animal is alarmed. Hair around the muzzle is usually silvery-white; head crest may be dark or dull chestnut in colour. Both sexes carry short, stout and partly ringed horns.

Similar Can only be confused with Abbott's duiker, but there is minimal range overlap and this species lacks yellow rump patch; see bushbuck, although very different from duiker.

Habitat Occur in most forest associations, as well as savanna woodland.

Behaviour A solitary forager; makes regular use of the same pathways within its home range. In some locations, several individuals may be seen in close proximity to one another, such as in forest glades. Although poorly known, it is likely that pairs mate for life and share the same home range and territory. Most activity takes place in the early morning and late afternoon hours, but they may be active at any time.

Food Wide range of fruit, berries, seeds, green leaves, fungi and moss.

Reproduction Probably no fixed breeding season within the region, but very little is known. Gestation said to be about 150 days, but probably longer, with the fawn weighing some 4 kg at birth.

Longevity 10 years in captivity.

Calls Sharp whistles when alarmed.

Occurrence Bwindi, Queen Elizabeth, Budongo (Uganda); Mt Elgon, Kakamega (Kenya). Very limited range in East Africa; is hunted, but status not clear.

MEASUREMENTS
Weight: 45–80 kg
Shoulder height: 65–85 cm
Total length: 1.26–1.6 m
Tail length: 11–18 cm
Record horn length (EA):
  15.88 cm (western Uganda)

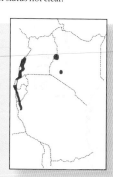

72

ADER'S DUIKER
Cephalophus adersi

Swahili: *Nunga* **German:** *Sansibarducker* **French:** *Céphalophe d'Aders*

Identification pointers Typical arched-back stance. Overall tawny-red colour becoming greyer on the neck, with off-white to white underparts. Easily identified by the white band across the buttocks and the white-spotting, or freckling, on the legs. Predominantly white, short tail. Sometimes placed with the red duiker complex of species. Both sexes carry short, spiky horns, on either side of a rufous-brown crest of hair.

Similar On Unguja (Zanzibar) see smaller suni; at Kenyan coast compare with red duiker, although lacking any white markings.

Habitat Forest, woodland and thicket, including dry scrub in coral rag country, known on Unguja as *msitu mkubwa*.

Behaviour Diurnal and lies up at night under cover. Normally solitary. Occasionally pairs and even trios (probably a ram, ewe and young of the season) are seen. Often follow troops of Zanzibar red colobus and Sykes's monkeys, picking up fallen plant food. The authors have seen a single duiker and a flock of crested guineafowl foraging below a tree in which several colobus were feeding. Mated pairs occupy marked territories.

Food A browser that selects for leaves, seeds and fruits.

Reproduction Nothing specific known, but young probably born at any time of the year.

Longevity Not known, but probably as for other similar-sized duikers.

Calls Alarm whistles.

Occurrence Threatened by habitat loss and hunting, with populations in the coastal forests of Kenya and Tanzania either extinct, or seriously threatened. On Unguja (Zanzibar), its last stronghold, there may be <1 000 individuals.

MEASUREMENTS
Weight: 6–12 kg
Shoulder height: 30–32 cm
Total length: about 75 cm
Tail length: 9–12 cm
Record horn length (EA):
  3.81 cm (Sokoke Forest, Kenya)

Front

30 mm

73

RED DUIKER
Cephalophus natalensis

Swahili: *Funo, Ngarombwi* **German:** *Rotducker, Harvey-Ducker* **French:** *Céphalophe du Natal, Céphalophe de Harve*

Identification pointers This duiker is difficult to separate in the field from *C. harveyi*, as well as Weyns' duiker (*C. weynsi*) (see map). Other similar species include Peters' (*C. callipygus*) and the black-fronted (*C. nigrifrons*). Overall body colour is rich reddish-brown to deep chestnut. Tail is tipped in black and white, and both sexes carry short, sharp, sloping horns. In *C. harveyi* there is a black facial blaze, the centre of the crest is black, and the legs may be somewhat darker.

Similar See Ader's duiker, but that species has very limited distribution and possibly close to extinction on mainland.

Habitat Most forest types and associated thickets, including on mountain slopes and in lowland.

Behaviour Diurnal; lies up under cover at night. Usually solitary animals are seen, but pairs may live in loose association in the same home range. Droppings are deposited in small heaps in specific areas that, along with glandular secretions, demarcate territory. Often feed on dropped items under trees in which monkeys and baboons are feeding. In some areas may reach quite high densities.

Food Wide range of plant food, including leaves, flowers, fruits and seeds. Opens hard monkey orange fruits by stabbing them with the horns against a rock or log. Like most duikers, also eats animal food: insects, birds, small mammals.

Reproduction Fawns, <1 kg, probably dropped at any time of the year, after a 210-day gestation.

Longevity 6 years captive, but possibly longer.

Calls Whistles and soft snorts.

Occurrence Selous, Mikumi, Mt Kilimanjaro (Tanzania); Masai Mara, Mt Kenya, Aberdares, Mt Elgon (Kenya); Queen Elizabeth, Murchison Falls (Uganda). Still quite common to abundant, but heavily hunted in some areas.

MEASUREMENTS
Weight: 10–16 kg
Shoulder height: 45 cm
Total length: 80 cm–1.1 m
Tail length: 9–15 cm
Record horn length (EA):
C. natalensis 10.48 cm (Mufindi, Tanzania); *C. harveyi* 12.7 cm (Elgeye Forest, Kenya)

Front

30 mm

■ *C. weynsi*
■ *C. harveyi*
■ *C. natalensis*

BLUE DUIKER

Cephalophus monticola

Swahili: *Ndimba* **German:** *Blauducker* **French:** *Céphalophe bleu*

Identification pointers The smallest duiker, with delicate appearance. Overall body colour variable, from pale slate-grey to dark brown, and this is largely regional, although it does vary somewhat within a population. Legs are typically a shade of brown, or brown-grey, usually contrasting with the body. Throat and chest often paler. Both sexes carry the short, sharp horns. Tail dark above and white below.

Similar See suni, as both about same size and both continuously flick the tail; ranges overlap in eastern Tanzania and on Unguja, Pemba and Mafia islands (Zanzibar archipelago).

Habitat Occupy probably the widest range of forest and wooded habitats of any other forest duiker. Rainforests to coastal dune forest, riverine and montane forest.

Behaviour Usually seen singly, but mated pairs occupy small, permanent territories. Secretions from the gland in front of the eye and tree-horning both serve as territorial markings. In prime habitat they occur at very high densities and can sustain a fair amount of hunting pressure. Said to be strictly diurnal, with most activity in the cooler morning and late afternoon hours. In areas of high disturbance they forage at night.

Food Primarily a browser, taking a mix of wild fruits, berries, fresh and fallen leaves, fungi; some animal food – mainly insects.

Reproduction Young born throughout the year; possible peaks. A single lamb, about 400 g, after 200-day gestation. Some authorities give the gestation as 165 days.

Longevity Possibly 10 years.

Calls Whistles, snorts and hoof stamping.

Occurrence Selous, Arusha, also main islands of Zanzibar archipelago (Tanzania); Mt Elgon (Kenya); Bwindi, Queen Elizabeth, Budongo (Uganda). Still common where they occur, despite heavy hunting.

MEASUREMENTS
Weight: 3.5– 6 kg
Shoulder height: 35 cm
Total length: 62–84 cm
Tail length: 7–12 cm
Record horn length (EA):
  7.3 cm (East Africa)

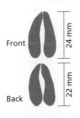

Front 24 mm

Back 22 mm

SAVANNA (AFRICAN) ELEPHANT

Loxodonta africana

Swahili: *Tembo, Ndovu* **German:** *Afrikanischer Elefant* **French:** *Eléphant d'Afrique*

Identification pointers Unmistakable, with vast size, long trunk, large ears and tusks. Tusks usually carried by bulls and cows; continue to grow throughout life. They never achieve full potential growth because of wear and breakage. Some animals, especially cows, may not develop tusks. Grey-brown skin usually hairless; takes on colour of local soil.

Similar No similar species.

Habitat Extremely wide habitat tolerance; includes coastal regions, lowland and montane forest, savanna associations, semi-desert and swamp.

Behaviour Matriarchal or family groups usually occupy home ranges of 15–>50 km² ; bulls may cover 1 500–3 120 km² (the latter recorded in Tsavo East). The small family herds consist of an older cow (the matriarch) and her offspring, with larger groups of related cows and calves. Herds number-ing in the hundreds may gather, but are usually temporary, and matriarchal herds maintain their integrity. Have complex means of communications including visual signs, touch, audible and sonic calls.

Food Very wide variety of plants and plant parts, including browse and grass.

Reproduction Single calf, about 120 kg, after 22-month gestation. Calves dropped throughout the year.

Longevity Up to 60 years in the wild.

Calls Rumbles, trumpeting, juvenile distress squeals, screams.

Occurrence Selous, Mikumi, Ruaha, Arusha, Serengeti, Ngorongoro, Mt Kilimanjaro, Lake Manyara, Tarangire, Katavi (Tanzania); Masai Mara, Amboseli, Tsavo, Shimba Hills, Aberdares, Mt Kenya, Meru, Mt Elgon, Marsabit, Samburu (Kenya); Queen Elizabeth, Murchison Falls, Kidepo (Uganda). Numbers and range have greatly declined, but they still occur widely in the region.

MEASUREMENTS
Weight: ♂ 5 000–6 500 kg;
♀ 2 800–3 500 kg
Shoulder height: ♂ 3.2–4 m;
♀ 2.5–3.4 m
Total length: ♂ 7–9 m; ♀ 6.5–8.5 m
Tail length: 1.5 m

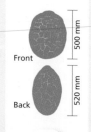

Front

500 mm

Back

520 mm

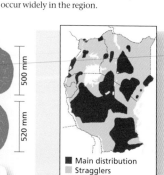

■ Main distribution
□ Stragglers

BAT-EARED FOX

Otocyon megalotis

Swahili: *Mbweha masikio* **German:** *Löffelhund* **French:** *Otocyon*

Identification pointers Small, jackal-like canid with slender legs and a sharp-pointed, fairly long muzzle. Ears are very large (14 cm), dark to black on the back surface and lined with a fringe of white hair on the inside. Body is covered in fairly long, silvery-grey hair with a grizzled appearance and the legs are black. Face has a silvery-white and black 'mask'. The bushy tail is black above and at the tip.

Similar Should not be confused with any other species, but see the 3 jackal species.

Habitat Open savanna country, savanna with short scrub, grassland and lightly wooded areas.

Behaviour Nocturnal and diurnal, largely depending on disturbance levels and in some areas influenced by the season. During the hottest hours they retreat to shade. Although they are capable of digging their own burrows, they usually take over and modify those dug by other species. Typically seen running in groups of 2–6 individuals, consisting of a pair that mate for life and their offspring of the season. When foraging they appear to wander aimlessly, stopping periodically with the ears turned to the ground.

Food Mainly insects, especially harvester termites, and numbers of small vertebrates. Wild berries are important at times.

Reproduction Pups in the region are dropped at the beginning of the rains when food is abundant. Litter of 1–6 (usually 2–4) pups, 100–150 g, dropped after 60–75-day gestation.

Longevity 13 years in captivity, but probably much less in the wild.

Calls Several very quiet calls seldom heard, chirping call from cubs in distress, growl/snarl combination, high-pitched bark.

Occurrence Serengeti, Ngorongoro, Lake Manyara, Ruaha, Tarangire (Tanzania); Tsavo, Amboseli, Masai Mara, Samburu, Nairobi (Kenya); Kidepo (Uganda). Still quite common.

MEASUREMENTS
Weight: 3–5 kg
Shoulder height: 30–40 cm
Total length: 75–90 cm
Tail length: 23–34 cm

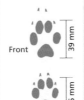

Front — 39 mm

Back — 36 mm

BLACK-BACKED JACKAL

Canis mesomelas

Swahili: *Mbweha nyukundu, Mbweha shaba* **German:** *Schabrackenschakal* **French:** *Chacal à chabraque*

Identification pointers Medium-sized, dog-like, with characteristic black saddle that is broad across the shoulders, narrows towards the tail base and is liberally sprinkled with white hairs. Face, flanks and legs pale to rich reddish-brown. Lips, throat and chest usually white (sometimes also underparts). Ears fairly large, pointed and reddish on back surface. Tail blackish; paler towards base.

Similar Side-striped jackal has white lateral stripe, shorter ears and a white-tipped tail; golden jackal has no distinctive markings.

Habitat Very wide tolerance; prefer drier areas, but occur in locations receiving more than 2 000 mm of rain.

Behaviour Nocturnal in areas where they come into conflict with humans; in undisturbed areas move and forage in cooler daylight hours. Mainly solitary or in pairs, but family parties not unusual. Pairs form a long-term bond and both mark and defend a territory. Range sizes vary according to factors such as food availability and disturbance. When rearing pups, a pair is often assisted by the young of the previous season.

Food Wide range of food: young antelope, rodents, birds, reptiles, insects and wild fruits. Carrion is readily eaten.

Reproduction Seasonal breeders (July to October) with litter sizes ranging from 1–8 pups, but usually 3–4, dropped after about 60-day gestation.

Longevity Rarely more than 7 years in wild; 14 years in captivity.

Calls One of the distinctive savanna calls: a screaming yell, finishing off with 3 or 4 sharp yaps, and often repeated.

Occurrence Serengeti, Ngorongoro, Tarangire, Mikumi, Ruaha (Tanzania); Marsabit, Samburu, Masai Mara, Nairobi, Tsavo (Kenya); Kidepo (Uganda). Still common and widespread.

MEASUREMENTS
Weight: 6–12 kg
  (♂ slightly larger)
Shoulder height: 30–48 cm
Total length: 71 cm–1.3 m
Tail length: 26–40 cm

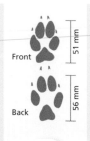

Front

51 mm

Back

56 mm

78

SIDE-STRIPED JACKAL

Canis adustus

Swahili: *Bweha* **German:** *Streifenschakal* **French:** *Chacal à flancs rayés*

Identification pointers From a distance, more or less uniformly grey, with legs often more brownish. At close quarters light-coloured stripe, or band, liberally fringed with dark grey or black, along each flank. Underparts and throat usually paler. Tail quite bushy, mostly black, usually with distinct white tip. Ears smaller than the other 2 jackal species.

Similar Black-backed jackal has saddle, different coloration; golden jackal has no lateral white stripe, dark tail tip.

Habitat Strong preference for well-watered and wooded areas, but not forest; avoids completely open areas. Recorded from sea level to altitude of 2 700 m.

Behaviour Mainly nocturnal, but may be active in the cooler daylight hours, or when overcast. Most sightings are of solitary animals, but pairs and family parties are not unusual. A home range and defended territory is occupied by a mated pair, and ranges seem to be well spaced. Unlike the other 2 jackal species, very little known.

Food The most omnivorous of the East African jackals; wide variety of food items: small mammals, birds, reptiles, insects, carrion, wild fruits, berries.

Reproduction 3–6 pups per litter, but birth seasons in East Africa not well known. In Uganda, litters recorded in June, July and September; most young observed in southern Kenya September/October. Reported gestation 57–70 days.

Longevity 10–12 years, but probably less in the wild.

Calls Most commonly heard at night is an owl-like hoot; explosive *bwaa*, cackling.

Occurrence Serengeti, Ngorongoro, Lake Manyara, Selous, Katavi (Tanzania); Tsavo, Masai Mara, Nairobi, Aberdares, Mt Kenya (Kenya); Queen Elizabeth, Murchison Falls, Lake Mburo (Uganda). Still widespread and common.

MEASUREMENTS
Weight: 7.5–12 kg
Shoulder height: 40–48 cm
Total length: 96 cm–1.2 m
Tail length: 30–40 cm

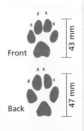

Front — 43 mm

Back — 47 mm

GOLDEN (COMMON) JACKAL

Canis aureus

Swahili: *Bweha wa mbuga* **German:** *Goldschakal* **French:** *Chacal commun*

Identification pointers Typical jackal-like appearance. Variable coat colour, usually pale golden-brown with a liberal sprinkling of black and grey hair on the back. Head, ears, flanks and lower legs are usually light brown to reddish-brown and underparts paler but never white. Tail is variably black, brown or grey, but always black-tipped.

Similar See black-backed and side-striped jackals.

Habitat Wide habitat tolerance, showing preference for open country with a scattering of trees and bushes.

Behaviour A mated pair occupies and defends a territory that in Serengeti studies ranged from 2–4 km², but may be larger in more arid areas of its range. A pair tolerates subadults from the previous litter as they help in the care and feeding of the current litter. Mainly diurnal, but in areas of disturbance they may switch to night-time activity. In areas of high food abundance, normal social structure may be disrupted and as many as 20 individuals may associate.

Food Omnivorous, taking fruits, small mammals, birds, reptiles and amphibians, as well as carrion. In the Serengeti, from January to February, Thomson's gazelle fawns and their afterbirths form an important component of their diet.

Reproduction In Tanzania most pups born January/February. Litters of 1–9 pups recorded, but 5–6 is usual. Gestation about 63 days; pups are weaned at 8–10 weeks.

Longevity 14 years recorded.

Calls A howling wail is the most frequently heard call, but also barks, growls, whines and cackles.

Occurrence Serengeti, Ngorongoro, Tarangire (Tanzania); Masai Mara, Samburu, Marsabit, Tsavo, Lake Turkana (Kenya); Kidepo, Queen Elizabeth (Uganda). Still common across its East African range.

MEASUREMENTS
Weight: 7–15 kg
Shoulder height: 38–50 cm
Total length: 80 cm–1.3 m
Tail length: 20–30 cm

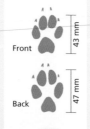

Front — 43 mm

Back — 47 mm

WILD DOG

Lycaon pictus

Swahili: *Mbwa mwitu* **German:** *Afrikanischer Wildhund* **French:** *Lycaon, Loup penit*

Identification pointers Similar in size to domestic German shepherd dog, although of lighter build and longer in the leg. Ears large, rounded and dark, and the bushy tail usually white-tipped. Body is irregularly blotched with black, white, brown and a yellowish-brown. Muzzle is black, with black continuing as a line from muzzle to between ears.

Similar Should not be misidentified, but see heavier and differently marked spotted hyaena; also see the jackals.

Habitat Open and lightly wooded savanna, moderately bushed country and, rarely, forest margins. Have been recorded at high altitudes on mounts Kilimanjaro and Kenya.

Behaviour Social, living in packs that average 10–15 adults and subadults. Packs include several related adult males, and 1 or more related adult female/s originating from different packs. Usually only the dominant pack female will successfully rear a litter of pups. Hunting is highly synchronised, with pack members working co-operatively. Nearly all hunting takes place during the day.

Food Medium-sized mammals, chiefly antelope. Thomson's gazelles and blue wildebeest are particularly important in the Serengeti and Masai Mara.

Reproduction In Serengeti 75% of litters are dropped between January and June. An average of 7–10 pups per litter are dropped after a 69–73-day gestation.

Longevity 10–11 years in wild, but in Selous most live only 6 years.

Calls Very vocal, with a range of calls; a far-carrying bell-like *hoo* hoot, barks, growls, bird-like twittering and whine.

Occurrence Selous, Serengeti, Ngorongoro, Mikumi, Ruaha (Tanzania); Masai Mara, Samburu, Tsavo (Kenya). Considered to be endangered as it has disappeared from much of its former range.

MEASUREMENTS
Weight: 17–25 kg
Shoulder height: 60–75 cm
Total length: 1.05–1.5 m
Tail length: 30–40 cm

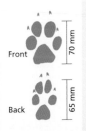

Front 70 mm

Back 65 mm

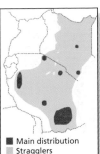

■ Main distribution
■ Stragglers

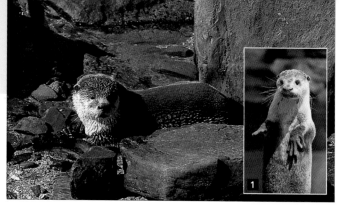

CAPE CLAWLESS OTTER

Aonyx capensis

Swahili: *Fisi maji* **German:** *Kap-Fingerotter* **French:** *Loutre à joues blanches*

Identification pointers Largest of the 2 otter species in East Africa. Coat is dark brown, but with white fur extending from the lips to upper chest. When wet, appears almost black. Legs short and stout; long tail is heavy at the base, tapers towards the tip. On land, walks with back arched. When swimming, usually only head visible. Toes finger-like and lack claws ▮.

Similar Spotted-necked otter much smaller and has white spotting on throat and upper chest. Range overlaps only in west of East Africa.

Habitat Rivers, estuaries, lakes, swamps and man-made dams. Frequently wanders several kilometres from water to move between suitable locations and to hunt.

Behaviour Mainly crepuscular, but activity has been recorded at all times of the day and night. Usually solitary, but also pairs and small family parties. At rest they lie up among dense vegetation or in self-excavated burrows (holts) in sandy soils adjacent to water-bodies. Latrine areas, with accumulations of whitish-grey droppings, useful indication of their presence. Much hunting in water relies on sight; also able to work in murky water by feeling with the sensitive fingers. Hunting on land is common.

Food Crabs, fish, frogs, as well as small mammals, birds, insects and molluscs. Molluscs are thrown at, or beaten against, rocks until the shells break.

Reproduction After a gestation of 60–65 days, 2–3 cubs are dropped. Estimated birth weight for pups is about 200 g.

Longevity A captive lived to 15 years.

Calls Broad vocabulary; aggressive, miaowing wail leading to a fierce *kwa-a-a-kwaaaaa* bark; contact whistles.

Occurrence In lakes Victoria, Tanganyika, Edward, George and others, and most river systems. Probably secure, but status difficult to establish.

MEASUREMENTS
Weight: 10–18 kg
  (max. 25 kg)
Shoulder height: 35 cm
Total length: 1.1–1.6 m
Tail length: 50 cm

Front

Back

106 mm

108 mm

SPOTTED-NECKED OTTER

Lutra maculicollis

Swahili: *Fisi maji* **German:** *Krallenotter, Fleckenhalsotter* **French:** *Loutre à cou tacheté*

Identification pointers Smallest of the East African otters, with a long, slender body and a somewhat flattened tail. Feet fully webbed; each toe carries a distinct claw. Overall body colour is dark brown to reddish-brown; blackish appearance when wet. Throat and upper chest variably mottled and/or blotched with white or creamy-white.

Similar See Cape clawless otter, which is much bigger and has uniform white throat; water mongoose similar size, but with shaggy hair and long-haired tail, and rarely swims.

Habitat Rivers, lakes, swamps, dams; unlike the Cape clawless it rarely moves far from water.

Behaviour A diurnal species that usually associates in groups of 2–6 animals, although larger groups have been seen. Quite vocal, group members maintaining contact with whistling calls. Droppings (smaller than those of the Cape clawless) are deposited in regularly used latrines close to the water's edge. Most prey is caught in the water and usually carried to the bank for eating. Rely mainly on sight for hunting; clear water is essential – they soon disappear from heavily silted waters.

Food Mostly fish, but they also take crabs, insects, frogs and birds.

Reproduction 2–3 cubs born after about 60-day gestation. They probably birth throughout the year, but on Lake Victoria young are said to be dropped in September.

Longevity Not known.

Calls Whistles, mewing *yea-ea-ea-ea*, squeaks and bird-like twittering.

Occurrence Fairly limited range in East Africa, but said to be common in lakes Victoria, Tanganyika and possibly Edward. Deaths in fishing nets may be quite high. Gombe Stream, Mahale (Tanzania); Queen Elizabeth, Murchison Falls (Uganda).

MEASUREMENTS
Weight: 3–5 kg
Shoulder height: <30 cm
Total length: <1 m
Tail length: 30–50 cm

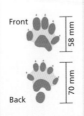

Front 58 mm
Back 70 mm

STRIPED POLECAT

Ictonyx striatus

Swahili: *Kicheche* **German:** *Zorilla* **French:** *Zorille commun*

Identification pointers Conspicuous black and white markings warn would-be predators that they can expect a squirt of foul-smelling liquid from its anal glands. Relatively long body hair is shiny black, with 4 distinct white stripes from top of head to base of tail along back and flanks. White patch on the forehead between the eyes, and a larger white patch at the base of the ear. Tail is predominantly white, but black shows through.

Similar Only the striped weasel (*Poecilogale albinucha*) in the far west of the region could be confused with it, though it is smaller, has very short legs and body hair, and top of the head is all white.

Habitat Very wide tolerance, and absent only from lowland forest.

Behaviour Strictly nocturnal, emerging only once it is dark. Usually solitary, but pairs and female accompanied by young sometimes seen. During the day they shelter in burrows dug by other species, among rocks, dense vegetation and even in association with man-made structures. When no other shelter available, capable of digging own burrows. Main defence is to spray foul-smelling fluid at an attacker; they also sham death.

Food Mainly insects and rodents, but also other small animals.

Reproduction Litter of 1–5 (usually 1–3) pups dropped after 36-day gestation. Not known in the region; likely that most births take place in the rainy months. Copulation may last for well over 1 hour.

Longevity 5.5 years in captivity.

Calls Has considerable repertoire: growls, bark-scream, high scream, etc.; seldom heard unless cornered or threatened.

Occurrence Present in most conservation areas. Very widespread in the region and able to adapt to human habitat modification. Frequently seen dead on roads.

MEASUREMENTS
Weight: 600 g–1.4 kg
Shoulder height: 10–15 cm
Total length: 57–67 cm
Tail length: 26 cm

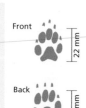

Front
22 mm

Back
22 mm

HONEY BADGER (RATEL)

Mellivora capensis

Swahili: *Nyegere* **German:** *Honigdachs* **French:** *Ratel*

Identification pointers Thickset, stocky and relatively short-legged, with short, bushy tail that is usually held erect when on the move. Upperparts are silver-grey, and underparts, legs and front of face are black. Usually a band of white separates upperparts from underparts, converging on top of the head and on down to the tail. Feet are large and powerful, with long claws on the front feet. Eyes are quite small and ears are tiny.

Similar Should not be confused with any other species in the region.

Habitat Found throughout East Africa, but possibly absent from arid north-eastern Kenya.

Behaviour Tough and potentially aggressive; has been recorded attacking species as large as elephant, buffalo and humans – but only when threatened. Usually seen singly, but pairs and family parties may be observed. Most activity takes place at night, but in undisturbed areas they may be seen in the cooler daylight hours, or when it is overcast.

Food Includes a wide range of invertebrates (insects, spiders, scorpions), but rodents, reptiles, birds, carrion and some wild fruits are also eaten. Their name comes from their tendency to break into beehives and eat honey and bee larvae.

Reproduction Usually 1–2 pups per litter, and often only 1 is successfully reared. Gestation is said to be about 62–74 days, although this is unconfirmed.

Longevity 26 years in captivity.

Calls Seldom heard, but a range of growls, screams, grunts, barks and whines.

Occurrence Serengeti, Ngorongoro, Selous, Mikumi, Ruaha, Mt Kilimanjaro, Katavi (Tanzania); Tsavo, Masai Mara, Meru, Samburu (Kenya); Queen Elizabeth, Murchison Falls, Kidepo (Uganda). Occurs everywhere at low densities.

MEASUREMENTS
Weight: 8–14 kg
Shoulder height: 30 cm
Total length: 90 cm–1 m
Tail length: 18–25 cm

Front

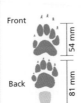

54 mm

Back

81 mm

AFRICAN CIVET

Civettictis civetta

Swahili: *Fungo, Ffungo* **German:** *Afrikanische Zibetkatze* **French:** *Civette*

Identification pointers Long-bodied, long-legged, heavily built; about the size of a medium dog (spaniel). When walking, head held low, tail usually horizontal or slightly drooping. Hair long and coarse, with a light grey forehead, white muzzle, and dark-ringed eyes. Distinct light band from the ear base towards the chest. Overall greyish to grey-brown, with many black spots, blotches and bands. Legs black. Tail banded white and black below, upperside and tip black. Ridge of dark erectile hair runs along spine to tail.

Similar Genets are smaller; shorter legs.

Habitat Wide tolerance, with preference for more densely wooded and forested areas, and nearly always close to water.

Behaviour Mainly nocturnal; but seen in cooler daylight hours in undisturbed areas. Foraging is solitary, but occasionally pairs seen, or a female and well-grown pups. Regularly used dung middens ('civetries') around their range; often located along paths and roadways. Also mark range with anal gland secretions, pasted on grass stalks, twigs and even rocks.

Food Mainly invertebrates, chiefly insects; also small rodents, hares, birds, reptiles, carrion and lots of wild fruits. Wild dates in large quantities in some areas.

Reproduction Birthing probably seasonal; 2–4 pups, after 60–65 days.

Longevity 15 years in captivity.

Calls Contact *ha-ha-ha*, cat-like meow, growls, cough-spit and scream. Seldom heard calling.

Occurrence Gombe Stream, Mahale, Katavi, Ruaha, Mikumi, Tarangire, Selous, Ngorongoro, Serengeti (Tanzania); Tsavo, Amboseli, Masai Mara, Lake Nakuru, Nairobi, Samburu, Mt Kenya, Aberdares, Marsabit (Kenya); Queen Elizabeth, Murchison Falls, Kidepo, Lake Mburo (Uganda). Widespread; fairly common, but never at high densities.

MEASUREMENTS
Weight: 9–15 kg
Shoulder height: 40 cm
Total length: 1.2–1.4 m
Tail length: 40–50 cm

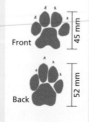

Front 45 mm

Back 52 mm

COMMON LARGE-SPOTTED GENET

Genetta maculata

Swahili: *Kanu* **German:** *Panther-Ginsterkatze* **French:** *Genette à grandes taches, Genette pardine*

Identification pointers Long, slender body with long tail, short legs and a fairly long, pointed snout. Quite large, thin, rounded ears. Tail thickly haired, banded black and white, with a dark-coloured tip . Coat colour varies from very pale to fawnish-yellow, with a liberal scattering of dark to rusty-brown spots and blotches. Underparts lighter, with no spots. Black and white markings on the face.

Similar Small-spotted genet differs in ground colour and has smaller spots, vertebral crest and usually white tail-tip. Civet much larger, longer in the leg and has proportionately shorter tail.

Habitat Associated with forest and woodland over much of the region.

Behaviour Strictly nocturnal, spending the day lying up under dense cover in tree holes. Forages readily on the ground, but moves freely in bushes and trees. Normally solitary, but occasionally seen in pairs, as well as female with young.

It is believed that females may hold, mark and defend territories. Droppings are deposited at latrine sites. Urine, scent-marking with anal glands and tree-scratching may serve to demarcate range.

Food Wide variety of invertebrates (mainly insects), mammals up to the size of hares, reptiles, frogs and birds. Some wild fruits.

Reproduction It is not known whether they are seasonal breeders in the region, but close to the equator they are probably not. Usually 2–5 young per litter, with pups weighing 50–80 g, born after gestation of about 70 days.

Longevity 14 years in captivity.

Calls Seldom heard, but various combinations of growling, coughs, spitting, purring and meowing.

Occurrence Still common and widespread, and found in most conservation areas where habitat is suitable.

MEASUREMENTS
Weight: 1.8–3.2 kg
Shoulder height: 18–22 cm
Total length: 85 cm–1.1 m
Tail length: 40–50 cm

Front — 22 mm
Back — 20 mm

SMALL-SPOTTED GENET

Genetta genetta

Swahili: *Kanu* **German:** *Kleinfleck-Ginsterkatze* **French:** *Genette commune*

Identification pointers Long, slender body and long, black and greyish-white ringed tail, usually with a white tip. Legs short. Long, rounded ears and rather pointed face with black and white markings. Crest of fairly long erectile hair runs from the nape to the base of the tail. Overall colour off-white to greyish-white, with numerous black spots and bars.

Similar Common large-spotted genet has different coat colour, larger and different coloured spots and no erectile crest. African civet much larger, longer legged, shorter tailed and fully terrestrial. On Unguja (Zanzibar) only servaline genet (*G. servalina*) occurs.

Habitat Very wide habitat tolerance, ranging from margins of arid areas to areas of high rainfall, but seldom in true forest. Mainly woodland, riverine margins, as well as isolated rock outcrops on open plains.

Behaviour Almost exclusively nocturnal, during the day lying up among dense vegetation, in rock crevices and burrows dug by other mammals. Perhaps more terrestrial than the other genets, but still an agile and able climber. Solitary; only rarely are pairs or females with young seen. Droppings deposited at latrine sites, usually on an exposed location such as a raised rock ledge or log, indicating that they serve to mark the home range.

Food Invertebrates (particularly insects) and will take small mammals, birds, reptiles, frogs and some wild fruits.

Reproduction 2–4 young, 50–80 g, after about 70 days, born in holes, rock crevices or dense vegetation tangles.

Longevity >9 years in captivity.

Calls Very similar to common large-spotted genet – cat-like call sequences.

Occurrence Occur in most reserves within its range. Common and widespread, even in areas of quite high human density.

MEASUREMENTS
Weight: 1.5–2.6 kg
Shoulder height: 18–20 cm
Total length: 86 cm–1 m
Tail length: 40–50 cm

Front

22 mm

Back

20 mm

SLENDER MONGOOSE

Galerella sanguinea

Swahili: *Kicheche* **German:** *Rotichneumon, Schlankmanguste* **French:** *Mangouste rouge*

Identification pointers Small, very slender and long-tailed; most races have a black-tipped tail, usually raised vertically or curved over the body when running. Colour ranges from dark brown, grey or fawn-brown to a deep chestnut-red **1**, but all should be recognisable as the slender mongoose. Fawn-brown or khaki-brown most commonly seen in the region. At least 16 races described from East Africa.

Similar Dwarf mongoose has shorter tail without black tip, and it engages in more social behaviour.

Habitat Areas of low and high rainfall, but usually absent from dense forest. Penetrate arid areas along watercourses and where there are stands of scrub and thicket. From sea level to at least 2 500 m. Reported to hunt in papyrus swamps.

Behaviour Usually solitary, but pairs run together for short periods during mating. Mainly terrestrial, but a capable climber: ascends into bushes and low trees with great agility. Stalk-and-pounce hunters, they approach very close to prey and lunge at it. Apparently strictly diurnal, lying up at night among dense vegetation, rock clusters or in holes dug by other animals. Probably territorial, with a male's territory overlapping those of several females.

Food May be regional differences, but take large quantities of rats and mice, insects, other invertebrates, reptiles, birds. Very occasionally wild fruits and berries.

Reproduction Litter of 1–2 (rarely 3) pups, after about 45-day gestation. Probably seasonal breeders – linked to the rains. On Unguja (Zanzibar), mating believed to take place in September.

Longevity Unknown.

Calls Seldom heard: harsh *tschaarrr* alarm growl, whine.

Occurrence Common in all reserves through its range in the region; frequently seen – often dashing across a road.

MEASUREMENTS
Weight: 370–800 g
Shoulder height: 10 cm
Total length: 50–65 cm
Tail length: 23–30 cm

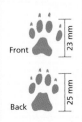

Front 23 mm

Back 25 mm

WHITE-TAILED MONGOOSE
Ichneumia albicauda

Swahili: *Nguchiro* **German:** *Weißschwanzmanguste* **French:** *Mangouste à queue blanche*

Identification pointers One of the largest mongooses in the area; walks with rump higher than the shoulder region and head usually held low. Legs are long, and when on the move the back is slightly arched. Coarse, shaggy hair is brown-grey, but the legs are black, and the bushy white tail is distinctive. In some populations, however, there are individuals with black tails.

Similar Jackson's mongoose (*Bdeogale jacksoni*) is very similar but shorter-haired and very rarely seen; occurs only in a limited area of central Kenya and adjacent Uganda.

Habitat Woodland savanna and forest margins are favoured, but they penetrate into drier areas along watercourses.

Behaviour Nocturnal and largely solitary, though pairs and female/young parties may be seen. In Serengeti, the average home range size was found to be 23–39 ha. Both sexes are territorial, although 2–3 females and their young may live in loosely knit clans. Lie up during the day in burrows dug by other species, or in rock crevices, holes in termite mounds, or among dense vegetation. Commonly enter gardens and forage around settlements in the region.

Food Insects and other invertebrates make up the most important part of its diet. Also hunts rodents, birds and reptiles; largest prey includes hares and cane-rats.

Reproduction Usually 1–2 young per litter (rarely 3–4), though birth season not well known. Most births probably coincide with the rains when food is most abundant.

Longevity 12.5 years in captivity.

Calls Muttering while foraging, whimpers, purs, growls, scream-shrieks, harsh barks.

Occurrence Present in most conservation areas; common through East Africa.

MEASUREMENTS
Weight: 3.5–5.2 kg
Shoulder height: 25 cm
Total length: 90 cm–1.5 m
Tail length: 35–48 cm

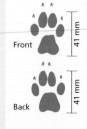

Front 41 mm

Back 41 mm

90

WATER (MARSH) MONGOOSE
Atilax paludinosus

Swahili: *Nguchiro cha maji* **German:** *Wassermanguste* **French:** *Mangouste des marais*

Identification pointers A large, stoutly built mongoose with a uniformly dark brown and rather shaggy coat. Some individuals may be almost black, or reddish-brown, but from a distance all look blackish and, at close quarters, grizzled. Hair on the muzzle and feet is short, but long and erectile on the tail.

Similar Could only be confused with Alexander's cusimanse (*Crossarchus alexandri*), but overlap may occur only in far-western Uganda; sometimes mistaken for otter, but latter is larger, sleeker and variably marked on throat.

Habitat Most well-watered habitats, rivers, marshes, swamps, lake fringes and coastline. Will penetrate arid areas along watercourses as long as permanent pools present. Sometimes found several kilometres from water.

Behaviour Nocturnal, crepuscular and terrestrial. Readily wade and swim. Probably territorial. Sightings are mainly of solitary animals, although pairs and females with young sometimes seen. When foraging they follow well-used pathways, and droppings are deposited at regularly used latrine sites – often near water. When hunting they rely on sight and hearing. Their long toes probe under and among rocks for prey.

Food Mainly crabs and amphibians, but also wide range of invertebrates, small rodents, birds; occasionally wild fruits.

Reproduction Births and young recorded in the region May to August, but are based on few records and are possibly aseasonal. Drop 1–3 cubs, about 120 g, in dense vegetation cover (reed beds), rock crevices, or the burrows of other species.

Longevity Not known.

Calls High-pitched bark alarm call is usually the only one heard.

Occurence Relatively common, but seldom seen.

MEASUREMENTS
Weight: 2.5–5.5 kg
Shoulder height: 22 cm
Total length: 80 cm–1 m
Tail length: 30–40 cm

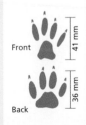

Front 41 mm

Back 36 mm

BANDED MONGOOSE

Mungos mungo

Swahili: *Nkuchiro* **German:** *Zebramanguste* **French:** *Mangue rayée*

Identification pointers Rather small, with very distinctive markings. Body colour varies from grizzled-grey to grey-brown, with 10–12 dark brown to black transverse bands on the back running from just behind the shoulders to the base of the tail. Fairly bushy tail and usually somewhat darker towards the tip. Head quite long and pointed, with rather short, rounded ears.

Similar Should not be confused with any other species.

Habitat Wide habitat tolerance, but does not occur in extremely dry areas (except along watercourses) or in forest. Shows a preference for woodland with adequate ground cover.

Behaviour Highly social, living in troops of 5–30 individuals and sometimes more. Strictly diurnal, spending nights in holes, especially in termite mounds, of which several are utilised within the home range. Range size varies according to number of troop members and food abundance, but studies have shown them to vary from 80 ha–>400 ha. Encounters between troops may result in conflict, but apparently they do not defend territories. Frequently mark rocks, logs and other troop members with the anal glands. When foraging, they retain contact with constant soft calls.

Food Mainly insects and other invertebrates, but also small vertebrates.

Reproduction Breeding usually synchronised within a troop. Averaging 20 g in weight, 2–6 young born after about 60-day gestation. Young may suckle from any lactating female. Most litters are dropped during the rains.

Longevity 11 years in captivity.

Calls Several distinctive calls, but the grunt-twitter *churr* is the most commonly heard when the troop is foraging.

Occurrence Common and widespread in many reserves in the region.

MEASUREMENTS
Weight: 1–1.6 kg
Shoulder height: 18–20 cm
Total length: 50–65 cm
Tail length: 18–25 cm

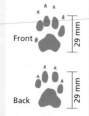

Front 29 mm

Back 29 mm

DWARF MONGOOSE

Helogale parvula

Swahili: *Kitafe* **German:** *Zwergmanguste* **French:** *Mangouste naine*

Identification pointers Along with the desert dwarf mongoose (*H. hirtula*) of far northern Kenya, this is the region's smallest mongoose. Fairly short but sleek, glossy coat, ranging from dark-brown to grey-brown; some have a reddish tinge; from close-up has a slightly grizzled appearance. Upper feet, throat and muzzle often more fawn to reddish. Tail same colour as body, well-haired but not bushy. No distinctive markings or contrasting colours.

Similar Slender mongoose has longer tail, with black tip – held erect or curved over body when running.

Habitat Open woodland and sparsely wooded savanna, as well as rocky areas within these habitats.

Behaviour Strictly diurnal and terrestrial; also highly social, living in troops of 10–40 individuals. A troop occupies a fixed home range of 2–30 ha. Within the range, each troop has up to 20 den sites, often within termite mounds, or among rocks. Every troop has a dominant male and female and – unusually – females are dominant over males. Usually only the dominant female breeds, but all troop members care for the young. Often sun-bask when they first emerge from the den. One of the most commonly sighted mongooses in East Africa.

Food Mainly insects, other invertebrates and to a lesser extent small reptiles, birds and their eggs.

Reproduction Births occur mainly during the rainy season, with litters of 1–7 (average 2–4) dropped after 50–54 days. Two litters annually is not unusual.

Longevity 7 years; 10 in captivity.

Calls Most commonly heard are *peep* and twitter contact calls; *tchee* and *tchrr* alarm calls.

Occurrence In many savanna reserves. Common and widespread over much of East Africa in suitable habitat.

MEASUREMENTS
Weight: 220–350 g
Shoulder height: 7 cm
Total length: 35–40 cm
Tail length: 14–20 cm

Front | 16 mm

Back | 16 mm

SPOTTED HYAENA

Crocuta crocuta

Swahili: *Fisi, Nyangao* **German:** *Tüpfelhyäne* **French:** *Hyène tachetée*

Identification pointers The most commonly seen hyaena, with heavily built forequarters that stand higher than rump. Large head, with prominent rounded ears and black muzzle. Colour ranges from fawn-yellow to grey-fawn, with a scattering of dark brown spots and blotches. Head, throat and chest not spotted. Tail is short and held erect or curved over the back at times.

Similar Striped hyaena has large, pointed ears, much longer vertebral mane, and black stripes on body and legs; also solitary.

Habitat Open and lightly wooded savanna, denser woodland types and rugged, broken country.

Behaviour Usually lives in family groups, or clans, led by an adult female. Clan size ranges from 3->15 individuals, with each clan defending a territory. Mainly nocturnal and crepuscular, although some daylight activity occurs. Skilled hunters, and will drive other predators from their kills. In and around reserve camps they will scavenge and can become a nuisance and dangerous.

Food Mainly antelope, but also plains zebra and buffalo.

Reproduction Usually 1–2 cubs (occasionally 3), born at any time of year, after gestation averaging 110 days.

Longevity >16 years in wild; 12–25 years in captivity.

Calls Among the most characteristic set of calls heard in savanna areas; *who-oop*, giggles, yells, growls, grunt-laughs, whines and soft squeals.

Occurrence Occurs in virtually all major reserves, including Selous, Mikumi, Ruaha, Katavi, Mahale, Serengeti, Ngorongoro, Tarangire, Lake Manyara (Tanzania); Tsavo, Amboseli, Masai Mara, Samburu, Marsabit (Kenya); Queen Elizabeth, Murchison Falls, Kidepo (Uganda). Numbers and range greatly reduced, but still widespread and common in conservation areas.

MEASUREMENTS
Weight: 60–80 kg
Shoulder height: 85 cm
Total length: 1.2–1.8 m
Tail length: 25 cm

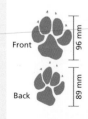

Front — 96 mm

Back — 89 mm

STRIPED HYAENA

Hyaena hyaena

Swahili: *Fisi* **German:** *Streifenhyäne* **French:** *Hyène rayée*

Identification pointers Distinctive sloping back of hyaena, with a rather shaggy coat that is buff to grey in colour and extensively marked with transverse black stripes. Legs are also well striped and ringed. Muzzle and throat are mainly black. A well-developed erectile mane extends from the base of the neck to the rump. Tail is fairly long and bushy, and ears are large and pointed.

Similar Should not be confused with any other species, but see much smaller aardwolf.

Habitat Drier areas, often found in association with rocky outcrops, and from savanna to desert.

Behaviour Most sightings are of solitary animals and occasionally pairs, with most activity taking place at night. During the day they may lie up in caves, under rock overhangs or among vegetation. It is believed they live in loosely associated groups within a common home range, although foraging is a solitary activity. Young from the previous litter may help care for the new litter. In Serengeti, home ranges of 2 animals were found to be 44 km² and 72 km².

Food Wide range of animal and plant food; scavenge readily.

Reproduction Usually 2–3 cubs in a litter, dropped after about 90-day gestation. Births may occur at any time of year. Cubs are dropped in a rocky den, or in a burrow taken over from another species.

Longevity 24 years in captivity.

Calls Not as vocal as spotted hyaena; whines, giggles, growls and yells.

Occurrence Serengeti, Ngorongoro, Tarangire, (Tanzania); Tsvo, Masai Mara, Samburu, Marsabit, Lake Turkana, Lake Bogoria (Kenya). Occurs at low densities, but probably not threatened.

MEASUREMENTS
Weight: <40–55 kg
Shoulder height: 72 cm
Total length: 1.2–1.55 m
Tail length: 25–35 cm

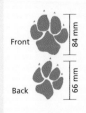

Front 84 mm
Back 66 mm

AARDWOLF

Proteles cristatus

Swahili: *Fisi ya nkole, Fisi mdogo* **German:** *Erdwolf* **French:** *Protèle*

Identification pointers Medium-sized, higher at the shoulders than rump, but this not as pronounced as in the 2 hyaenas. Coat is coarse and longish, and there is a mane of erectile hair on the neck and back, which is raised when the animal is under stress. Colour ranges from pale tawny to yellow-white and there are several vertical black stripes on the body, and black bands on the upper part of the legs. Muzzle, feet and much of the tail are black. Ears are large and pointed.

Similar Striped hyaena much larger, with proportionally shorter tail.

Habitat Very wide tolerance, from low to high rainfall, with range dependent on availability of its principal food – termites.

Behaviour Mainly nocturnal and crepuscular, but active on overcast days in undisturbed areas. Normally a solitary forager, but on occasion pairs and family parties seen. Two or more animals occupy a home range, with droppings deposited in shallow scrapes at latrine sites and anal gland secretions deposited on grass stalks. Several females may drop their pups in the same den, usually in burrows excavated by other species, but if not available they will dig their own.

Food Termites, especially harvesters, make up the bulk of their diet but also some other insects and, very rarely, small vertebrates.

Reproduction Drop 1–4 pups after a gestation of about 90 days. Most births probably occur during the rains.

Longevity 15 years in captivity.

Calls Seldom heard, but if cornered or injured give an impressive roar; barks and growls.

Occurrence Serengeti, Ngorongoro, Ruaha (Tanzania); Masai Mara, Samburu, Tsavo, Marsabit (Kenya). Nowhere common, but not generally threatened and in some areas they benefit from overgrazing by livestock.

MEASUREMENTS
Weight: 6–11 kg
Shoulder height: 50 cm
Total length: 84 cm–1 m
Tail length: 20–28 cm

Front

Back

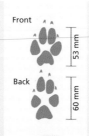

53 mm

60 mm

CARNIVORES

CHEETAH

Acinonyx jubatus

Swahili: *Duma* **German:** *Gepard* **French:** *Guépard*

Identification pointers Often called the 'greyhound' of cats, with its slender body and long legs that are suited to high speed. Head is small, with short muzzle and a clear black line (tear-line) running from the inner corner of each eye to the corner of the mouth. Overall body colour off-white to pale fawn and liberally dotted with more or less uniformly sized rounded black spots. Long tail is spotted and black-ringed and usually has a white tip.

Similar Leopard heavier, with rosettes not spots, no tear-line; serval smaller, notably shorter tail, large ears, no tear-line.

Habitat Open country, plains, grassland and wooded grassland.

Behaviour Normally seen singly, in pairs, or in small family parties of a female and her cubs. Adult males move singly or in small bachelor coalitions of related animals. Females establish territories and drive out other females. Males not as territorial; may move over the ranges of

several females. In Serengeti, and probably elsewhere, females have much larger ranges than males. Mainly day-active; rely on rapid (>70 kph) dashes when hunting.

Food Favours medium-sized mammals, especially antelope up to about 60 kg. Thomson's gazelle is important in the Serengeti/Masai Mara. Hares sometimes taken, as well as birds to size of ostrich.

Reproduction 1–5 cubs (usually 3–4), weighing 250–300 g, dropped at any time of the year, but peaks occur in some areas. Gestation about 92 days.

Longevity 17–21 years in captivity.

Calls *Chirrup* and *churr* contact calls; *nyam nyam* and *ihn ihn* when female calls cubs; growls, snarls, spits and purrs.

Occurrence Serengeti, Ngorongoro, Selous, Ruaha, Tarangire (Tanzania); Masai Mara, Amboseli, Tsavo, Samburu, Meru, Marsabit (Kenya); Kidepo (Uganda). Range and numbers greatly reduced and now mainly in conservation areas.

MEASUREMENTS
Weight: 30–72 kg (most 40–60 kg)
Shoulder height: 80 cm
Total length: 1.8–2.2 m
Tail length: 60–80 cm

Front 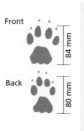 84 mm

Back 80 mm

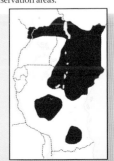

LEOPARD

Panthera pardus

Swahili: *Chui* **German:** *Leopard* **French:** *Léopard*

Identification pointers Powerfully built cat; colour ranges from off-white to orange-russet; black spots on legs, flanks and head. Spots over rest of body consist of rosettes or broken circles of irregular black spots. Tail about half of total length, white-tipped, with rosette spots above. Ears rounded and white-tipped.

Similar Cheetah has slender build, longer legs, solid spots, a black tear-line from eye to mouth; serval much smaller, with shorter tail, larger ears, solid spots.

Habitat Coastal plains to high-altitude mountains, semi-desert to rain forest.

Behaviour Solitary cat, except when a pair meet in order to mate, or a female is accompanied by cubs. Often night-active, but in areas where they are not hunted or disturbed daytime activity is not unusual. Primarily terrestrial, but they climb and swim well. Adult males mark and defend a territory and a male's range may overlap those of several females. Territories marked with droppings, urine scrapes and sprays, tree-scratching and calling. They are stalk-and-pounce hunters.

Food Can utilise a very wide range of animal food, from insects to large mammals. Most prey is small to medium-sized antelope, but in some areas rock hyrax and hares are important. In areas where other large predators occur, prey is usually lodged in trees.

Reproduction Litters of 2–3 cubs, each weighing about 500 g at birth, are born after about 100-days' gestation. Births may take place at any time of year.

Longevity 21 years in captivity.

Calls Most commonly heard is a territorial 'wood-sawing' call, with 13–16 strokes of a 'saw' in about 12 seconds, repeated every few minutes (usually 5–8).

Occurrence Occur in all of the region's major reserves. Some decline in numbers and range, but still common and widespread in East Africa.

MEASUREMENTS
Weight (EA): ♂ 37–90 kg; ♀ 28–60 kg
Shoulder height: 70–80 cm
Total length: 1.6–2.1 m
Tail length: 68 cm–1.1 m

Front — 92 mm

Back — 92 mm

LION

Panthera leo

Swahili: *Simba* **German:** *Löwe* **French:** *Lion*

Identification pointers Largest of the East African cats. Body colour ranges from pale tawny to reddish-grey, with paler underparts. Faint spotting is present on cubs, particularly on the sides, and sometimes retained by adults. Tail same colour as body, and has tip tuft of dark brown to black hair. Adult males carry manes of long hair, normally extending from sides of face onto neck, shoulders and chest.

Similar Unmistakable.

Habitat Desert fringes to woodland and fairly open grassland. Primarily a species of the savannas.

Behaviour Sociable, living in prides of 3–30 individuals. Each pride consists of a stable core of related females, their dependent offspring, and usually a coalition of 2 or more adult males (sometimes just 1). Young males disperse from the birth pride and form coalitions. When new males take over a pride, they usually kill younger cubs. Most hunting is undertaken by the lionesses, mainly at night, or during cooler daylight hours.

Food Mainly medium-sized to large mammals, especially ungulates. They will chase other predators from their kills.

Reproduction No fixed breeding season, usually 1–4 cubs, about 1.5 kg, after 110-day gestation. Pride females allow any cub to suckle from them.

Longevity 13–15 years; 30 captive.

Calls Lion roar starts with a few low moans, followed by 4–18 very loud roars, and ends with an average of 15 grunts. Full roars can be heard for up to 8 km. Other calls are commonly associated with social interactions and kills.

Occurrence Best numbers in Serengeti, Ngorongoro, Selous, Ruaha, Mikumi, Tarangire (Tanzania); Tsavo, Masai Mara, Samburu (Kenya); Kidepo, Queen Elizabeth, Murchison Falls (Uganda). Numbers and range greatly reduced outside reserves.

MEASUREMENTS
Weight: ♂ 150–225 kg;
♀ 110–152 kg
Shoulder height: ♂ 1.2 m; ♀ 1 m
Total length: ♂ 2.5–3.3 m;
♀ 2.3–2.7 m
Tail length: 1 m

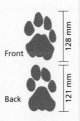

Front 128 mm

Back 121 mm

SERVAL

Leptailurus serval

Swahili: *Mondo, Kisongo* **German:** *Serval* **French:** *Serval*

Identification pointers Slender, long-legged, spotted cat with short tail and large, rounded ears. Body colour variable, but usually yellowish-fawn with scattered black spots and bars. Black bars and spots on neck. Black bands extend down the legs. Underparts paler, but usually also spotted. Back surface of ear has black band, separated from black tip by white patch. In some high-altitude areas, such as the Aberdares, all-black specimens are quite common.

Similar Much smaller than leopard and cheetah; both have longer tails.

Habitat Usually areas with water, tall grassland, reed beds and forest fringes.

Behaviour Often nocturnal, but in protected areas commonly seen during the cooler daylight hours. Mainly solitary, but sightings of pairs and family groups not unusual. Largely terrestrial, but they are agile climbers. The male is territorial; may well apply to the females as well. One male in Ngorongoro had a home range of 7.5 km² and a female 4 km². Ranges overlap; serval density may be quite high, but contact within ranges is minimal.

Food Variety of small mammals, especially rodents, and birds make up the bulk of their diet.

Reproduction Litters are usually dropped during the rains, with 1–5 (usually 2–3) cubs dropped, each weighing about 200 g. The gestation is 68–79 days.

Longevity 13–20 years in captivity.

Calls Range of snarls, growls and purrs, but seldom heard.

Occurrence Serengeti, Ngorongoro, Tarangire, Ruaha, Gombe Stream, Mahale (Tanzania); Tsavo, Masai Mara, Samburu, Marsabit, Aberdares, Mt Kenya (Kenya); Queen Elizabeth, Murchison Falls (Uganda). Still quite common in reserves where habitat is suitable, but has been wiped out in areas of higher human population.

MEASUREMENTS
Weight: 8–13 kg
Shoulder height: 60 cm
Total length: 96 cm–1.2 m
Tail length: 25–38 cm

Front 47 mm

Back 44 mm

CARACAL

Caracal caracal

Swahili: *Simbamangu* **German:** *Karakal* **French:** *Caracal*

Identification pointers A robustly built medium-sized cat; hindquarters stand higher than shoulders. Ears black-backed, with sprinkling of white hairs, long and pointed, with tuft of longish black hair at tips. Coat is short, dense and soft, with colour ranging from pale yellowish-fawn to rich brick red. Underparts may be slightly paler to almost white. Prominent black and white patches on the face, especially around mouth and eyes. Short tail is same colour as body.

Similar Golden cat, but largely separated by habitat.

Habitat Semi-desert to open and woodland savanna, from low to high rainfall areas and sea level to montane regions. It enters some less closed forest types.

Behaviour Mainly nocturnal, but where undisturbed will hunt during the cooler daylight hours. Solitary, mainly terrestrial but can climb well. Males are territorial and their home ranges overlap those of 1, 2 or more females. Not known in region but elsewhere ranges of 4–>100 km² recorded. They are crouch-and-pounce hunters.

Food Small to medium-sized mammals, from mice to 40 kg antelope, birds and, rarely, reptiles. In some areas hyrax are important in their diet.

Reproduction Seasonal birth-peaks are likely but not known in region. After 79-day gestation 1–3 kittens, weighing about 250 g, are born.

Longevity 17 years in captivity.

Calls Typical cat-like calls, loud coughs, growls, spitting hisses, miaows.

Occurrence Ngorongoro, Serengeti, Katavi, Ruaha, Mikumi (Tanzania); Tsavo, Masai Mara, Aberdares, Mt Kenya, Marsabit (Kenya); Kidepo (Uganda). At low densities over much of East Africa, but not threatened.

MEASUREMENTS
Weight: 7–19 kg
  (♂ larger than ♀)
Shoulder height: 40–45 cm
Total length: 70 cm–1.1 m
Tail length: 18–34 cm

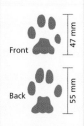

Front — 47 mm

Back — 55 mm

GOLDEN CAT

Profelis aurata

Swahili: – German: *Goldkatze* French: *Chat doré*

Identification pointers Medium-sized, robust cat with dark-backed, rounded ears. Colour is commonly red-brown, but some animals are dark brown or greyish. Dark spots are present to a greater or lesser extent on the underparts, and occasionally over entire body. Underparts and inner legs usually off-white to white. Tail only about a third of total length.

Similar See caracal, but latter's ears are pointed and tufted; differ in main habitat requirements. Leopards share habitat, but are larger and more clearly spotted, with longer tails.

Habitat Tropical and montane forests, but extends into adjacent woodland; also high-altitude alpine moorland. Will also occupy secondary forest growth.

Behaviour Probably solitary, but pairs have been observed. Little is known of species in the wild. Usually hunt on the ground, although believed to be at least partly arboreal. Active both at night and during the day, in the latter case probably depending on level of disturbance. They are stalk-and-pounce hunters.

Food Rodents, hyrax and duikers probably make up much of their diet; also hunt birds, e.g. guineafowl and francolin.

Reproduction Very little known, but may den down in trees, among dense foliage or in caves. Very similar, and better known, Asian golden cat (*Profelis temmincki*) has 1–3 young per litter after 80-day gestation, each kitten averaging 250 g in weight.

Longevity 17–20 years in captivity for Asian golden cat; African probably similar.

Calls Growls, snarls and other typical cat-like calls. Rarely heard.

Occurrence Restricted to a few forest and montane areas in Uganda and south-west Kenya. Ruwenzori, Queen Elizabeth, Bwindi (Uganda); Aberdares, Mt Kenya (Kenya).

MEASUREMENTS
Weight: 8–16 kg
Shoulder height: 38–50 cm
Total length: 1.07–1.35 m
Tail length: 35–45 cm

ROCK HYRAX
Procavia capensis

Swahili: *Pimbe, Pimbi* **German:** *Klippschliefer* **French:** *Daman de rocher*

Identification pointers Small, stoutly built and tailless, with short legs. Overall colour is variable, but mainly light to dark brown. Hair length also variable: animals living at higher altitude have fairly long, shaggy coats; those at lower altitudes are more sleek. They have a gland in the centre of the back surrounded by longish, black, brown or yellowish erectile hair.

Similar Yellow-spotted rock hyrax (*Heterohyrax brucei*) very similar and shares range of this species, but is greyer and has pale yellow dorsal spot; tree hyraxes (*Dendrohyrax* spp.) in some montane areas live among rocks, including on Unguja (Zanzibar) and their dorsal spot is usually pale yellow or white.

Habitat Mainly mountain and hill ranges, as well as isolated rock outcrops.

Behaviour Diurnal, living in colonies of 4–8 individuals, but in favourable habitat their densities may be very high. They sun-bask in the early morning for a lengthy period then move off to feed. Each colony has a strict pecking order and a dominant male and female. Rarely move more than a few hundred metres from the home shelter. Heavily hunted by larger eagle species, caracal, leopard and humans; seem able to sustain the heavy offtake. Populations periodically crash; believed to be associated with disease.

Food Variety of plant parts, especially leaves, buds and flowers. During times of food shortage, will eat tree bark.

Reproduction Young, 1–3, rarely up to 5, are well developed at birth and weigh 150–300 g. Gestation about 210 days.

Longevity 12 years.

Calls Sharp alarm bark, often ending in a wheeze; chatters and snarls during interactions.

Occurrence Common and very widespread (as is the yellow-spotted) in most reserves where there is suitable habitat in low- and high-rainfall areas.

MEASUREMENTS
Weight: 2–5 kg
Shoulder height: 15–30 cm
Total length: 40–60 cm

Front
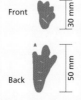
30 mm

Back
50 mm

YELLOW-SPOTTED ROCK HYRAX

Heterohyrax brucei

Swahili: *Pimbe* **German:** *Buschschliefer* **French:** *Daman gris*

Identification pointers Very similar to rock hyrax in overall form, but slightly smaller; head narrower and often lighter in colour – but not in all cases. Hair in the centre of the back is off-white to yellowish and there is often a white patch above each eye. Underparts are usually paler to white.

Similar Very similar to rock hyrax and often shares habitat; but dorsal gland hair of latter is usually dark to black. Often sun-bask and huddle together. Generally separated from tree hyraxes by habitat.

Habitat Mainly mountainous and hilly country, including isolated rock outcrops lying on open plains such as those found in Serengeti.

Behaviour Mainly diurnal with most feeding taking place in the morning and late afternoon. Climb readily into trees to feed. Live in small colonies, but in suitable habitat may live at high densities – 20–53 animals per ha. Each colonial group consists of a dominant male, females and their young of up to 2 years. Seldom move as far from shelter as the rock hyrax.

Food Predominantly browsers; much of their feeding is done in trees and bushes, taking very little grass or low herbage. This is in contrast to the rock hyrax, thus reducing feeding competition between the 2 species.

Reproduction May be aseasonal, or strongly seasonal. In Serengeti there are 2 birth-peaks (May to July and December to January); around Nairobi peak occurs in February to March. After about 230-day gestation, a litter of 1–3 young is usual.

Longevity >10 years in captivity and possibly also in the wild.

Calls Shrill alarm bark; male territorial bark-rattle. Within colony twitters and chunters.

Occurrence Common; occur in many parks and reserves.

MEASUREMENTS
Weight: 1.3–4.5 kg
Shoulder height: 15–30 cm
Total length: 32–56 cm

Front

Back

30 mm

50 mm

TREE HYRAX

Dendrohyrax spp.

Swahili: *Perere* **German:** *Baumschliefer* **French:** *Daman d'arbre*

Identification pointers Small, stoutly built and tailless, with short legs. Head longish with short, rounded ears. Overall colour variable – usually shades of brown, grey-brown and, in some cases, almost black; underparts paler to white. In centre of back a longer-haired, lighter coloured dorsal spot – cinnamon (*D. validus*) **1**, creamy-white (*D. arboreus*), or long and pale to white (*D. dorsalis*). Hair length may vary in different populations.

Similar Very similar to rock and yellow-spotted rock hyrax; usually separated on habitat choice; but in some areas tree hyrax are ground dwellers, and rock hyrax may readily climb in bushes and trees.

Habitat A range of forest, including montane, woodland and thicket types. In some areas, such as the Ruwenzori (*D. arboreus*) and Unguja and Pemba (Zanzibar Archipelago) (*D. validus*), they live among rocks and on latter they live among coral rag. Some species overlap in the region. Sea level to 4 500 m.

Behaviour Mainly nocturnal but sun-basking not uncommon. During the day they shelter in tree holes, among dense vegetation and in rock crevices. Mainly solitary, in pairs or family groups, but in favourable habitat their densities may be very high. Feed chiefly in trees and bushes but also on the ground.

Food Wide range of plants, including leaves, twigs, bark, flowers and fruits.

Reproduction Largely aseasonal breeders, but there may be birth-peaks in some cases. After about 210-day gestation 1–3 well-developed young (rarely 5), 150–300 g, are dropped.

Longevity >10 years in captivity.

Calls Hair-raising rattling and screaming diagnostic; only at night.

Occurrence Common in many suitable areas. *D. validus* is only hyrax on Unguja and Pemba islands (Zanzibar Archipelago).

MEASUREMENTS
Weight: 2–3.5 kg
Shoulder height: 15–30 cm
Total length: 40–60 cm

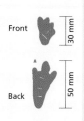

Front — 30 mm

Back — 50 mm

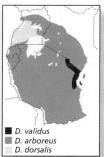

■ *D. validus*
▨ *D. arboreus*
▨ *D. dorsalis*

AARDVARK

Orycteropus afer

Swahili: *Muhanga, Kukukifuku* **German:** *Erdferkel* **French:** *Oryctérope*

Identification pointers With its long, pig-like snout, elongated tubular ears, kangaroo-like tail and powerful, stout legs it resembles no other East African mammal. The body is sparsely covered with coarse, bristle-like hairs and those on the base of the tail and legs are usually darker in colour. Overall colour is generally grey-fawn, often tinged with the colour of the local soil. Back is distinctly arched; walks with shambling gait.

Similar Should not be mistaken, but see the warthog and bushpig.

Habitat Prefers open woodland, sparse scrub and grassland, but can be expected in most habitats, including forest.

Behaviour Predominantly nocturnal, but at times forages during the cooler daylight hours and periods of severe drought. Nearly always solitary animals seen, except if a female is accompanied by a youngster. Dig extensive burrow systems and occupied ones are often characterised by numerous small flies in the entrance. When foraging, they appear to wander aimlessly until an ant or termite colony is encountered and they then tear into it with the massive claws on the front feet.

Food Mainly ants and termites; ants often more important in the dry season.

Reproduction Single young, weighing about 2 kg, dropped after some 210-days' gestation. Mating may be linked to onset of the rains.

Longevity 18 years in captivity.

Calls Subdued grunts when foraging; calf-like bellow if frightened or in pain.

Occurrence Serengeti, Ngorongoro, Tarangire, Katavi, Selous, Ruaha, Mikumi (Tanzania); Tsavo, Masai Mara, Nairobi, Meru, Mt Kenya, Aberdares, Lake Bogoria, Samburu, Marsabit (Kenya); Queen Elizabeth, Murchison Falls, Lake Mburo (Uganda). Widespread, but nowhere common.

MEASUREMENTS
Weight: 40–70 kg
Shoulder height: 60 cm
Total length: 1.4–1.8 m
Tail length: 45–60 cm

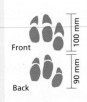

Front

100 mm

Back

90 mm

GROUND PANGOLIN
Manis temmincki

Swahili: *Kakakuona* **German:** *Steppenschuppentier* **French:** *Pangolin terrestre du Cap*

Identification pointers Covered with large scales over back, sides and tail. Curls into ball to protect unscaled belly if frightened . Has tiny pointed head and powerfully developed hind legs and tail. Small forelegs are rarely used for walking.

Similar There are 3 other pangolin species in the region: much larger (30–35 kg) but similar giant ground pangolin (*M. gigantea*) found in forests and moist grassland in Uganda; long-tailed and white-bellied tree pangolins (*M. tetradactyla* and *M. tricuspis*) are arboreal, have proportionally much longer tails and occupy rain forests in Uganda and far western Kenya.

Habitat Dry woodland savanna.

Behaviour Predominantly nocturnal, but some crepuscular activity, and will forage on overcast days. Although it will excavate its own burrow, it will use those dug by other species, or lie up among dense vegetation. Burrows may be closed from the inside when occupied. They are solitary, except when a female is accompanied by the single young – which clings to her back at the base of the tail when she is foraging.

Food Certain species of ants and termites, their eggs and larvae.

Reproduction Probably breeds throughout the year in East Africa; may be more seasonal in drier areas. Single young, 330–450 g, after about 140 days.

Longevity Not known, a giant pangolin said to have lived just 4 years in captivity. Probably live longer than this, as are difficult to keep in captivity.

Calls Generally silent, but make snuffling noises when foraging.

Occurrence Serengeti, Ngorongoro, Selous, Ruaha, Gombe Stream, Mahale, Tarangire (Tanzania); Marsabit, Masai Mara, Tsavo (Kenya); Kidepo (Uganda). Uncommon to rare, but widespread in the region.

MEASUREMENTS
Weight: 5–18 kg
Total length: 70 cm–1.1 m
Tail length: 30–50 cm

Back

60 mm

■ Ground pangolin
■ Giant ground pangolin

FOUR-TOED SENGI (ELEPHANT SHREW) *Petrodromus tetradactylus*

Swahili: *Isanje* **German:** *Vierzehenrüsselratte* **French:** *Pétrodrome à quatre orteils*

Identification pointers A large sengi, with hind legs and feet considerably longer than the front, a long, slender and mobile snout, and fairly long membranous ears. The coat is soft and dense, buff-coloured above and with slight orange or reddish-brown tinge. Underparts are whitish and often with yellow or orange tinge on flanks. White ring around large eye.

Similar Larger than the other 2 sengis in region, but smaller than the 4 giant sengi species. Snout separates it from any local rodents of similar size.

Habitat Occupy areas with dense vegetation including thickets around rock outcrops, closed woodland, riverine forest, as well as drier coastal and montane forest.

Behaviour Pairs probably occupy and defend territories. Within each territory (average 1.2 ha in one Kenyan study) there is a network of paths that are patrolled regularly and kept clear of debris such as leaves. Characteristic of these pathways are bare patches every 40–100 cm resulting from their bounding gait – not caused by jumping on hind legs as sometimes thought. Active at night but also during the morning and late afternoon.

Food Mainly insects, including termites and ants.

Reproduction Probably breed at any time of the year and the usual 1, occasionally 2, young are well-haired and active shortly after birth.

Longevity A captive individual lived for 6 years 7 months.

Calls Shrill squeak; drums on ground with hind feet and tail.

Occurrence Quite common in the region and in many reserves and parks. Hunted in some areas, but this is not a serious threat to survival of the species.

MEASUREMENTS
Weight: 160–280 g
Total length: 35 cm
Tail length: 16 cm

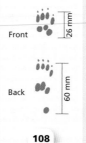

Front — 26 mm

Back — 60 mm

GOLDEN-RUMPED SENGI

Rhynchocyon chrysopygus

Swahili: *Njule* **German:** *Goldsteiß-Rüsselhündchen* **French:** *Rhynchocyon*

Identification pointers One of perhaps 5 species of giant sengi in the region. Very large – much bigger than other sengis. Moves with somewhat arched back and resembles miniature duiker. Elongated head and snout, and a rat-like tail. Hind legs and feet much longer than front. Golden-rumped has distinctive straw-coloured patch on rump, with rest of upperparts deep reddish and black. Most other giant sengis have greater or lesser amount of chequering on back.

Similar See smaller four-toed sengi, but these have no distinctive back markings.

Habitat Occupy dense, moist coastal scrub and adjacent lowland forest and woodland. Other giant sengis occupy mainly forested associations.

Behaviour Diurnal and spend the night in a shallow cup excavated in soil and then lined and covered with dead leaves, in which they hide. Live in pairs on defended territories, with male chasing away male, and female seeing off female. Average territory size is 1.7 ha and they may reach high densities.

Food Insects make up much of their diet; probably also take other invertebrates such as snails and earthworms.

Reproduction Breed throughout year; single young dropped after about 42-day gestation. First 2 weeks spent in leaf nest on forest floor. Other giant sengi species apparently give birth to 2 young.

Longevity 4–5 years; one captive individual lived >11 years.

Calls Squeals and squeaks; drumming with tail and probably with hind feet.

Occurrence Golden-rumped endangered because of habitat loss and hunting; Peters' giant sengi from coastal Kenya and Unguja, Mafia Islands (Zanzibar Archipelago) also under serious threat. Golden-rumped occur in Arabuko-Sokoke, Gedi Ruins (Kenya).

MEASUREMENTS
Weight: 400–550 g
Total length: 43–56 cm
Tail length: 20–26 cm

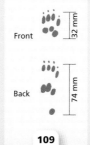

Front — 32 mm

Back — 74 mm

R. reichardi
R. petersi
R. stuhlmanni
R. chrysopygus
R. udzungwensis

SHORT-SNOUTED SENGI

Elephantulus brachyrhynchus

Swahili: *Sengi* **German:** *Kurznasen-Elefantenspitzmaus* **French:** *Macroscélide à nez court*

Identification pointers A small sengi that has reddish-brown fur on upperparts and greyish-white underparts; tail comparatively shorter and thickened. Despite common name, snout not greatly shorter than in other *Elephantulus* species. Narrow white ring around eye.

Similar Similar but darker *E. fuscipes* only in northern Uganda; *E. rufescens* has somewhat longer snout and very distinct white eye-ring.

Habitat Mainly found in dry woodland, thickets and areas with adequate cover.

Behaviour Active during daylight hours and apparently forage during even the hottest hours but usually remain within shade. Rarely move more than 20 m from shelter, which may be among rocks, in other animals' burrows or in termite mounds. Small pathways may radiate from the shelters to feeding sites. Mainly solitary and in small groups, but in optimum habitat may reach quite high densities. Males appear to be territorial.

Food Take a wide range of insects and other invertebrate prey, but also feed on some fruits and seeds.

Reproduction Possibly breed through the year, as pregnant females recorded in November and June in Kenya, but may be linked to rainy seasons in some areas. Twins more common than single young and they are well developed at birth. In common with other species, young probably weigh about 10 g at birth after possible 50-day gestation.

Longevity A captive individual lived for 4 years 2 months.

Calls Squeals during aggression; drums tail and hind feet.

Occurrence Common; found in most conservation areas within region.

MEASUREMENTS
Weight: 44 g (average)
Total length: 18–26 cm
Tail length: 8–12 cm

Front — 7 mm

Back — 16 mm

SPECTACLED (RUFOUS) SENGI

Elephantulus rufescens

Swahili: *Sange mdogo* **German:** *Rote Elefantenspitzmaus* **French:** *Macroscélide rouge*

Identification pointers Typical sengi with long, cylindrical snout, long, membranous ears and hind legs and feet longer than front. A distinctive bright white ring around the eye, usually with a dark stripe running from back of eye to base of ear. Variable in coat colour with most Kenyan animals being rufous, in north-western Tanzania more grey and in remainder of Tanzania yellowish-fawn.

Similar Short-snouted sengi has shorter tail; range overlap occurs only in some areas.

Habitat Occupy dry acacia scrub country and thickets growing on well-drained soils. Not uncommon around rural villages where there are hedges that provide cover.

Behaviour A mated pair share a territory of about a third of a hectare, but forage mainly alone. Males drive off males, and females chase away females.

In areas of optimum habitat, several pairs may live in fairly close proximity. Most activity takes place during the day and they forage along established paths that radiate from resting areas. Mainly shelter under and among dense vegetation where they dig shallow scrapes to lie in.

Food Mainly insect eaters but probably also take some plant food.

Reproduction The few records indicate that they may give birth to 1 or 2 young, weighing about 10 g, after an estimated 62-day gestation, at any time of year. A female may have several litters in a year.

Longevity In wild one lived for 1 year 7 months; a captive lived 7 years and 11 months.

Calls Squeals and foot drumming.

Occurrence Present in many parks and reserves within range. Widespread and generally common.

MEASUREMENTS
Weight: 25–50 g
Total length: 20–30 cm
Tail length: 10–16 cm

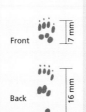

Front   7 mm

Back   16 mm

WHITE-BELLIED HEDGEHOG

Atelerix albiventris

Swahili: *Kalunguyeye* **German:** *Weißbauchigel* **French:** *Hérisson à ventre blanc*

Identification pointers Unmistakable, with dorsal covering of short, sharp, banded spines. Underparts and much of face covered with coarse white hair. When threatened or alarmed, roll into tight ball with spines protecting face, belly and legs. Ears quite short and rounded; legs short.

Similar Only hedgehog in region. Sometimes confused with much larger and longer spined/quilled porcupine.

Habitat A wide range of habitats but avoids areas with very high rainfall and wetland communities. Favours dry thickets and scrubland country; not uncommon in some suburban settings, such as Nairobi and Tabora.

Behaviour Mainly nocturnal, but may be seen on cool, overcast days. Solitary foragers commonly seen, but pairs and females with young may be encountered. This species is poorly known, but it probably bears many similarities to other hedgehog species. During the dry season, when food availability is reduced, it apparently becomes less active and may remain in shelter for several weeks.

Food Capable of eating a third of its body weight in a night, the hedgehog has to eat large quantities of insects, earthworms, snails, slugs and small vertebrates. Some plant food may be taken, but this is poorly understood.

Reproduction After about 40-days' gestation, 2–10 young (average 5), weighing between 8 and 18 g, are dropped. Young are independent by about 40 days of age.

Longevity The European hedgehog (*Erinaceus europaeus*) lives to 7 years and white-bellied probably similar.

Calls Range of grunts, snorts and sniffs.

Occurrence Occurs in many reserves and parks and probably still secure.

MEASUREMENTS
Weight: 270–700 g
Total length: 19–28 cm
Tail length: 2–5 cm

Front — 18 mm

Back — 22 mm

WHITE-TOOTHED (MUSK) SHREWS

Crocidura spp.

Swahili: *Kirukanjia* **German:** *Weißzahnspitzmäuse* **French:** *Crocidura*

Identification pointers Number of shrew species in East Africa unknown: certainly more than 60, possibly many more. The largest group, the white-toothed shrews, number at least 50 species; most, if not all, are hard to identify. All are small, mouse-sized mammals, with long, wedge-shaped snouts and short legs. Most white-toothed shrews have sparse, long bristles on tail. Short, soft coats may be grey, black, fawn or brown; teeth are wholly white.

Similar Difficult to separate from other shrew genera, but only the small *Suncus* shrews also have longish tail bristles. Can be confused with some of smallest rodents, such as pygmy mouse.

Habitat Different species occupy virtually all East African habitats from swamps to high mountains, coastal dunes to forest, deserts to high rainfall areas. More than 1 species may be found in any given area.

Behaviour Alternating periods of activity and rest throughout a 24-hour period. Those species studied defend territories within fixed home ranges. Mainly solitary, but in the most suitable areas they may occur at high densities. Some live in short burrows; others construct nests in dense vegetation.

Food Insects make up the bulk of their prey; also a range of other invertebrates such as earthworms, snails and spiders.

Reproduction Little studied in the region, but litters of 2–6 naked, helpless young are dropped after about 18 days. Most species probably not seasonal breeders. Depending on species, young may weigh as little as 1 g at birth.

Longevity Up to 4 years in captivity.

Calls Twittering when foraging; sharp squeaks.

Occurrence A few species very localised and may be threatened, but others widespread and common.

MEASUREMENTS
Weight: 6–40 g
Total length: 10–20 cm
Tail length: 3–9 cm

Front

Back

11 – 21 mm

from to

113

STRAW-COLOURED FRUIT-BAT
Eidolon helvum

Swahili: – **German:** *Palmenflughund* **French:** *Rousette des palmiers africaine*

Identification pointers Largest bat on the African mainland. It has a dog-like face, large reddish-brown eyes and prominent rounded ears. Wings are long and tapered and dark brown to black in colour. Body colour is variable from dull yellow/grey-brown to rich yellowish-brown, with paler underparts. Hindquarters and limbs usually darker than rest of body. Tail very short.

Similar Egyptian fruit-bat smaller and dull dark-brown to greyish-brown. Epauletted fruit-bats have distinctive white hair tufts at ear bases and on shoulders.

Habitat A species mainly of tropical forest, but disperses at times into other habitats throughout East Africa where there is abundant fruit.

Behaviour In some areas form into vast roosts numbering hundreds of thousands, but outside the tropics smaller numbers are usual. Roosts are often located in suitable trees within urban areas. Even within large colonies they usually hang in clusters of 10–50. Roosts are noisy and smelly, with animals jockeying for prime locations. They leave for the feeding grounds after sunset and may fly several kilometres in search of fruiting trees.

Food Eat a wide range of both wild and cultivated fruits.

Reproduction Records from Uganda show that most young are born from February and into March. Single young (rarely twins), weighing 40–50 g, born after about 120 days. Mother carries young with her when foraging for up to 6 weeks.

Longevity >21 years in one case.

Calls Wide range of squeals, screams, and chattering at roost; usually quiet in flight. Noise levels can be extreme in large colonies.

Occurrence Still occur in large numbers but disturbance of colonies is a growing problem, for example, at the roost in Kampala, Uganda.

MEASUREMENTS
Weight: 230–350 g
Wingspan: 75 cm
Total length: 19 cm
Tail length: 4–20 mm

■ Main distribution
■ Migrants

EPAULETTED FRUIT-BATS

Epomophorus spp.

Swahili: *Nema* **German:** *Epaulettenflughunde* **French:** *Epomophorus*

Identification pointers At least 6 species occur in the region and all have fox-like heads and white tufts of hair at the base of the ears. Males have white-haired shoulder pockets – the epaulettes that give the group its name. Overall body colour varies from light to dark brown. When the pouch is spread, white hair is prominent. It is difficult to separate the different species in the field.

Similar No other fruit-bats have the white ear tufts and epaulettes.

Habitat Occupy forest and riverine woodland, but will extend into drier woodland. Some species even roost in trees along busy roads in towns.

Behaviour Most species roost in small numbers in trees or bushes, but several hundred may gather in suitable locations. It is not unusual for them to roost under open roofs of buildings. They leave their roosts after sunset and may fly several kilometres to feeding grounds. Some species undergo migrations in search of more productive fruiting trees, but this is poorly understood.

Food Mainly soft wild and cultivated fruits; at least some, if not all, feed from tree flowers. Fruit pulp is chewed, juice is swallowed, but pips and pulp are spat out.

Reproduction Some species may breed at any time of year, whereas others could be seasonal in some areas. Single young are usual, but twins have been recorded. Young of *E. labiatus* are recorded as weighing an average 11 g, whereas larger species drop young of up to 20 g.

Longevity Not known.

Calls Chuckle, squeal and squeak while feeding; males make a repetitive clinking call.

Occurrence One or other species occurs in most parks and reserves. Some species are common and widespread, with a few being rare. Disturbance at some roosts may be a problem.

MEASUREMENTS
Weight: 40–160 g
Wingspan: 45–60 cm
Total length: 12–25 cm

from

to

COMMERSON'S LEAF-NOSED BAT
Hipposideros commersoni

Swahili: – German: *Commerson-Rundblattnase* **French:** *Hipposideros*

Identification pointers One of the largest insect-eating bats in Africa and could be confused with the fruit-bats. It has a distinctive but simple skin structure on the nose, the 'nose-leaf', and the ears are large, pointed and leaf-like. The hair is short and soft, variable in colour from sandy-brown to grey-brown; underparts are lighter to white. The male has a white patch on the shoulder.

Similar Large size could lead to confusion only with fruit-bats, but the latter have dog-like heads and distinctive calls.

Habitat Savanna woodland and forest, but they also penetrate into quite arid areas, particularly along watercourses.

Behaviour Roost in colonies of hundreds of individuals, hanging free in clusters but not in contact with neighbours. Daylight hours spent in caves, also large hollow trees and, rarely, hanging in exposed undergrowth. When disturbed at roost, can crawl rapidly over the surface to escape into crevices. They are rather slow but agile fliers.

Food Take a variety of insects, especially beetles in some areas; also termites. Often return to a feeding perch to consume larger prey. They have been recorded as removing beetle larvae from figs. Most food is taken in flight and at low levels from the ground.

Reproduction Births have been recorded in December and they are possibly seasonal breeders. Only single young are on record.

Longevity Not known, but only sexually mature at 2 years.

Calls Shrill, clearly heard, alarm call.

Occurrence Common. Not seriously threatened, although hunted in parts of region for their meat.

MEASUREMENTS
Weight: 75–180 g
Wingspan: Up to 60 cm
Total length: 15 cm

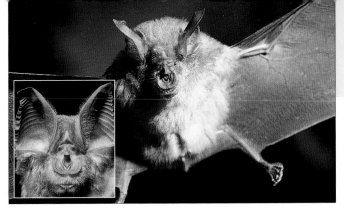

HORSESHOE BATS

Rhinolophus spp.

Swahili: − German: *Hufeisennasen* **French:** *Rhinolophe*

Identification pointers About 10 species of horseshoe bat occur in East Africa, all easily recognisable as such, but very difficult to identify to species level. All are characterised by the elaborate nose-leaves over the face between the mouth and forehead, which help in their identification. They have squared tails and quite large ears that lack a tragus (skin extension). Colour varies from species to species and sometimes within a single species, but most are various shades of brown or grey-brown.

Similar In the hand should not be confused as nose-leaves are distinctive.

Habitat Many species associated with savanna woodland but can be encountered in most habitats.

Behaviour Some species roost in small numbers; others such as Geoffroy's may come together in thousands. All principally cave roosters, but mine shafts and dark corners of buildings also serve the purpose. Hang free by their feet, singly or in well-spaced groups, wings enfolding the body. Most insect-eating bats roost with wings folded at their sides. The broad, round-tipped wings allow for slow, butterfly-like flight; most, if not all, have hunting territories.

Food Generally low-flying hunters: take a wide range of flying insects such as moths and beetles, but some species will snatch invertebrates from the ground.

Reproduction Very little known in East Africa; seems some species have more restricted breeding seasons than others. All probably have single young.

Longevity No records in region; a European horseshoe bat (*R. ferruequinum*) lived for at least 24 years.

Calls At frequencies rarely audible to human ears.

Occurrence Poorly known but probably none threatened in region.

MEASUREMENTS
Weight: 4–27 g
Wingspan: 20–40 cm
Total length: 7–11 cm

smallest

largest

SLIT-FACED BATS

Nycteris spp.

Swahili: – **German:** *Schlitznasen* **French:** *Nyctères*

Identification pointers Recognisable by the long, lobed slit down the centre of the face; when slit open the nose-leaves clearly visible. Have large, more or less straight- and parallel-sided ears. Wings broad, rounded at the tips. T-shaped tail-tip strongly characteristic. In East Africa 7 species occur – a few widespread and common, others rare and little known. Coat variable from dark brown, grey-brown to russet; underparts always paler.

Similar The 2 long-eared bats in region are the heart-nosed bat (*Cardioderma cor*) and the yellow-winged bat (*Lavia frons*); have very different nose-leaf structures.

Habitat Some species have wide habitat tolerance (from areas with high rainfall to near-desert); others prefer specific habitats, e.g. forest/forest fringes.

Behaviour Most species roost in small numbers and are often found roosting alone or in pairs. Some, e.g. Egyptian slit-faced bat (*Nycteris thebaica*), may gather in hundreds. Roosts include caves, buildings and dense vegetation. All are slow but highly efficient fliers. Most prey taken on the wing; will also snatch invertebrates off the ground. Larger prey is taken to a regularly used perch to eat. Perches identifiable by accumulations of non-edible parts such as moth wings.

Food Insects and other invertebrates make up much of their prey, but the large slit-faced bat (*Nycteris grandis*) also takes small fish and frogs.

Reproduction Little known in region, but at least some may be seasonal breeders (although a female may give birth several times in a year). Mothers carry young when hunting at night.

Longevity Unknown for region.

Calls High frequency calls very rarely heard by humans.

Occurrence Some species common and widespread, others little known and considered rare.

MEASUREMENTS
Weight: 11–40 g
Wingspan: 24—35 cm
Total length: 9–16 cm

smallest
largest

118

EGYPTIAN FREE-TAILED BAT

Tadarida aegyptiaca

Swahili: – **German:** *Bulldoggfledermaus* **French:** *Tadarida*

Identification pointers About 25 species of free-tailed bats recorded in East Africa; difficult to identify except as a group. However, easily identified individually as free-tailed bats. The tail is free and only half, or less, is enclosed by the narrow interfemoral membrane. Also known as bulldog, mastiff or wrinkle-lipped bats, for their dog-like faces and the wrinkled upper lip. Coat hair short and velvety in shades of brown to blackish. Wings usually narrow and long. Give off strong rubbery smell at roosts.

Similar In the hand should not be confused with any other bat group because of its partly free tail and wrinkled lips.

Habitat 1 or more species occupy most habitats in the region. Favour open woodland and river courses; also semi-arid and high-rainfall areas. Egyptian free-tailed bats occur in most drier habitats.

Behaviour May form into roosts of hundreds, in caves, rock crevices, hollow trees and behind loose bark of dead trees. May also form substantial colonies in buildings. Unlike other bats they can scuttle rapidly along the ground. When hunting, they tend to fly high and rapidly. An American species was recorded flying as high as 3 000 m.

Food A wide range of insects, including moths and beetles. The authors have watched these bats on the ground snatching emerging termite alates.

Reproduction Despite abundance, very little known; in the south of the range drop single young in summer months. Unlike several other species, they leave the young at the roost and do not carry them.

Longevity No African records exist. A South American species lived for 8 years.

Calls High-frequency chitter.

Occurrence This species common and widespread, but several other free-tailed bat species considered rare.

MEASUREMENTS
Weight: 15 g
Wingspan: 30 cm
Total length: 11 cm
Tail length: 3.8 cm

EAST AFRICAN SPRINGHARE

Pedetes surdaster

Swahili: *Kamendegere* **German:** *Springhase* **French:** *Lièvre sauteur*

Identification pointers Despite its name, this is a true rodent and not a hare. Resembles a small wallaby, with long and well-developed hind legs and a hopping gait. Front legs are very short and are used only for digging out its food. Tail is long, bushy and black towards the tip. The ears are quite long, and its eyes are noticeably large. Upperparts are yellowish or reddish-fawn, but underparts are paler to white.

Similar See true hares; though they move on all 4 feet, their ears are very much longer, and their tails are black and white and short.

Habitat Compacted sandy soils with short vegetation cover.

Behaviour Strictly nocturnal, terrestrial and not territorial. Unlike its southern relative, this springhare occupies communal burrow systems. They dig 2 types of burrow: a sloping one with considerable amounts of sand around the entrance, and a vertical, clean, escape burrow. Occupied burrows are often blocked with sand from the inside. In areas of prime habitat they can occur in large numbers, and in agricultural regions they can become a nuisance.

Food Grass, grass roots and other plants, as well as cultivated crops.

Reproduction Single young, weighing approximately 300 g, is well developed at birth, but remains in the burrow for the first 6–7 weeks of life. In East Africa, young may be born at any time of year, but at least in parts seasonal peaks may occur.

Longevity 8 years in captivity.

Calls Normally silent, but gives soft grunts on feeding grounds.

Occurrence Hunted by a wide range of predators, including humans, but still common, although localised because of habitat needs.

MEASUREMENTS
Weight: 2.5–3.8 kg
Total length: 75–85 cm
Tail length: 35–45 cm

Left   Right

38 mm

SOUTHERN PORCUPINE
NORTH AFRICAN PORCUPINE

Hystrix africaeaustralis
Hystrix cristata

Swahili: *Nungu* **German:** *Stachelschwein* **French:** *Porc-épic*

Identification pointers Large size and long, black and white banded quills and spines diagnostic. Both occur in East Africa, with much range overlap in Tanzania; separated in the field with great difficulty. Flanks, neck, head and underparts have dark, coarse hair. Crest of long, erectile, coarse hair runs from top of head to shoulders. Crest, quills and spines raised when animal is alarmed.

Similar Can only be confused with forest-dwelling brush-tailed porcupine (*Atherurus africanus*) in Uganda and marginally in western Kenya, but that species has shorter quills that are not as clearly banded, and its tail is longer.

Habitat Wide; often favours rocky areas.

Behaviour Strictly nocturnal, spending the day in burrows (excavated itself or taken over from another species), or in rock crevices, caves and even among dense vegetation. A feature of regularly used porcupine dens is an accumulation of bones, gnawed on to prevent overgrowth of incisors. In home range, uses regular pathways, typically showing signs of its foraging. Several porcupines may share a den, but foraging is solitary.

Food Roots, bulbs, corms, tubers and tree bark are favoured; also eat some wild fruits, and crops, e.g. potatoes, pumpkins.

Reproduction Litters of 1–4 (usually 1–2) young, weighing 100 to 300 g (up to 450 g unusual), are well developed at birth; quills harden in the second week.

Longevity Possibly 20 years.

Calls When alarmed/threatened, rattle hollow tail quills and stamp hind feet; soft grunts when foraging, or when 2 or more animals meet; generally silent.

Occurrence In virtually all East African reserves. Common in many areas and widespread, but regularly hunted as a pest and for its meat.

MEASUREMENTS
Weight: 10–24 kg
Shoulder height: 25 cm (>45 cm when quills raised)
Total length: 75 cm–1 m
Tail length: 10–15 cm

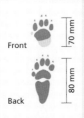

Front

70 mm

Back

80 mm

WESTERN GROUND SQUIRREL
Xerus erythropus

Swahili: *Kindi, Kidiri* **German:** *Gestreiftes Borstenhörnchen* **French:** *Écureuil fouisseur*

Identification pointers Squirrel-form with long and bushy tail, coarse sandy coloured coat with a distinctive white stripe running from shoulder to mid-flank. Underparts paler to white and legs often more brown. Ears are very short and eye is ringed in white.

Similar Unstriped ground squirrel where ranges overlap – see map; the latter lacks white side stripes.

Habitat Fairly wide range but favour semi-arid areas with sparse and open vegetation, including woodland.

Behaviour Dig their own burrows but also live in termitaria and in rocky areas in crevices and holes. May form loose colonies but usually only 1 animal per retreat. They are solitary foragers. Commonly associated with the fringes of cultivated lands and may cause damage to crops. Diurnal and terrestrial, they frequently stand on their hind legs scanning their surroundings. The bushy tail is sometimes used as a sunshade.

Food Dig for roots, grass seeds and leaves, fallen fruits, nuts; *Acacia* pods also eaten. Will take a variety of cultivated crops. Also take insects, especially termites, as well as some vertebrate prey.

Reproduction Little is known. They probably breed throughout the year, although most young are apparently dropped from August and into October. Usual litter consists of 2–6 pups, with an average of 4.

Longevity Up to 6 years in captivity.

Calls An excited chatter, typically squirrel-like.

Occurrence Lake Mburo, Murchison Falls, Kidepo (Uganda); Tarangire (Tanzania); Samburu, Amboseli (Kenya). No known threats and common in some areas.

MEASUREMENTS
Weight: 500–950 g
Total length: 48–72 cm
Tail length: 18–26 cm

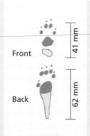

Front — 41 mm

Back — 62 mm

UNSTRIPED GROUND SQUIRREL

Xerus rutilus

Swahili: *Kindi, Kidiri* **German:** *Ostafrika-Erdhörnchen, ungestreiftes Borstenhörnchen* **French:** *L'Écureuil unicouleur*

Identification pointers Plain-coloured, ground-dwelling squirrel, with a bushy tail and small, rounded ears. Coat colour is variable, but usually reddish-brown and heavily pencilled with white. Underparts are much paler, from creamy-fawn to almost white. The tail is a mix of brown, black and white hairs. Front feet have long claws.

Similar In south-west Kenya and Uganda it is replaced by the western ground squirrel (*X. erythropus*), and their ranges overlap in parts of Kenya and north-eastern Tanzania. It is somewhat larger than *X. rutilus* and has a distinctive white stripe along each side.

Habitat Relatively dry habitats, and does not occur in areas of high rainfall, more favoured by the western ground squirrel. Occupies areas from sea level to about 2 000 m above sea level.

Behaviour Strictly diurnal and terrestrial, with individual burrow systems isolated from each other. Dig their own burrows, with 2–6 entrances, even in hard soils, using the long claws on the front feet. Burrows are often located under dense scrub, in thickets and even in cut-brush used to construct cattle enclosures. In suitable habitat they can reach very high numbers: in 1 study up to 848 individuals per km².

Food Seeds, wild fruits, roots, pods.

Reproduction Poorly known, but 1–2 young seems to be the norm.

Longevity A male caught in the wild lived for >6 years in captivity.

Calls Not known, but like other ground squirrels probably largely silent.

Occurrence Tsavo, Amboseli, Meru, Samburu, Marsabit, Lake Turkana (Kenya); Kidepo (Uganda). Common throughout its range.

MEASUREMENTS
Weight: 260–420 g
Total length: 32–44 cm
Tail length: 12–22 cm

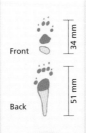

Front

34 mm

Back

51 mm

TREE (SMITH'S BUSH) SQUIRREL

Paraxerus cepapi

Swahili: – **German:** *Smith-Buschhörnchen* **French:** *Écureuil de Smith*

Identification pointers Small, with typical squirrel-like appearance, bushy tail and no distinguishing markings. Coat colour is grizzled sandy or greyish or yellow-brown, with lighter to white-coloured underparts. In the south-east of Tanzania they interbreed with the red bush squirrel (*Paraxerus palliatus*) and hybrids may be brighter coloured than typical tree squirrels.

Similar Red bush squirrel with red belly and undertail found in eastern range; ochre bush squirrel (*Funisciurus ochraceus*) in north-east has sandy grizzled-ochre coat and side stripe; striped bush squirrel (*F. flavivittis*) has grizzled coat and broad white stripe down sides and is found in south-east Tanzania. The two sun squirrels (*Heliosciurus* spp.) occur across tree-squirrel range and have ringed tail in east, and red-coloured legs.

Habitat A variety of woodland types but not true forest.

Behaviour Usually seen singly or in mother/young groups, but several animals live in loose association. The adult male, or males, in a group will defend a territory against outside squirrels. Diurnal and will forage in trees and on the ground.

Food Wide variety of plant food as well as insects. Surplus food may be cached for later use.

Reproduction After about a 55-day gestation 1–3 young are dropped in a leaf-lined tree hole, with average weight of pups 10 g. Most litters occur in summer, but little further is known in region.

Longevity Not known.

Calls Harsh chattering scold, usually with tail flicking.

Occurrence Common, occurring through southern Tanzania including Katavi, Ruaha, Selous, Mahale.

MEASUREMENTS
Weight: 100–260 g
Total length: 29–36 cm
Tail length: 15–18 cm

Front

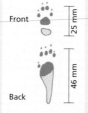

25 mm

46 mm

Back

BARBARY STRIPED GRASS MOUSE
Lemniscomys barbarus

Swahili: *Panya* **German:** *Berber-Streifengrasmaus* **French:** *Souris rayée de Barbarie*

Identification pointers A smallish mouse with brown to dark brown fur. Numerous pale stripes extending from shoulders to rump on either side of a dark to black stripe running down centre of back. In most populations the backs of the ears are reddish-brown. These attractive rodents are also known as zebra mice.

Similar In the 2 other *Lemniscomys* species in East Africa the many white lines are broken into dashes and dots; a single-striped species (*L. griselda*) is also widespread across the region. The four-striped grass mouse (*Rhabdomys pumilio*) is found only in higher altitude areas of the region.

Habitat Open and drier savannas with dense grass cover and scattering of low shrubs and trees.

Behaviour Live in loose groupings, but do not seem to be particularly social, although in optimal habitat they may reach quite high densities. Construct small, round nests on, or close to, the ground and well-defined paths radiate from them. Paths are often not visible as they run under grass cover. Mainly nocturnal and crepuscular, but there is some daytime activity.

Food Range of seeds, green plant material and sometimes insects, especially termites.

Reproduction Breeding in the region is tied to the seasonal rains, and females may have several litters during this time. Usually 4–5 young, each weighing about 3 g, are dropped after a 28-day gestation.

Longevity Not known but probably <3 years.

Calls Squeaking – rarely heard and only when handled.

Occurrence They are common and widespread; in most parks and reserves in their range.

MEASUREMENTS
Weight: 23–40 g
Total length: 19–24 cm
Tail length: 9–13 cm

Front

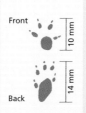

Back

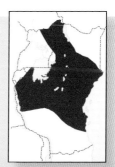

PYGMY MOUSE

Mus minutoides

Swahili: – **German:** *Afrikanische Zwergmaus* **French:** *Souris naine d'Afrique*

Identification pointers Very small, delicate mice with tail shorter than head and body length, fairly prominent and rounded ears and sometimes a small white patch at ear base. Upperparts range from light fawn to dark russet-brown with some black hair pencilling. Underparts and upper foot surfaces usually clean white.

Similar At least 3 additional species of pygmy mice occur in East Africa, but some authorities recognise many more. All are small and very similar in appearance as are most aspects of their behaviour. Some call the pygmy mouse in the region *M. musculoides*. The small climbing mice (*Dendromus* spp.) differ in having tails that are longer than head and body, with a narrow black line down the centre of the back.

Habitat Wide range of habitats – from low to high rainfall, sea level to montane regions.

Behaviour Nocturnal and terrestrial. May be solitary, in pairs or in family parties. During periods of ideal conditions they may reach high densities. Commonly associate with larger rodent species, making use of their runways and possibly benefiting from their food wastage. Can dig their own burrows but readily use those of other species, or shelter under dense vegetation, debris or rocks.

Food Mainly seeds and green plant material but also some insects.

Reproduction After a gestation period of just 19 days litters of 1–7 (usually 4) young are dropped. Young helpless at birth and weigh <1 g. Probably breed year-round with possible seasonal peaks.

Longevity One record in captivity claims just over 3 years.

Calls Quiet twittering.

Occurrence Common and found in many parks and reserves.

MEASUREMENTS
Weight: 2.5–10 g (average 6 g)
Total length: 10 cm
Tail length: 4 cm

WOODLAND THICKET RAT

Grammomys dolichurus

Swahili: – **German:** *Akazienmaus* **French:** *Grammomys*

Identification pointers Long tails well over half their total length; ears quite long and rounded. Upperparts may be reddish-brown with a grey tinge or more greyish-brown, and underparts are white. Rump area often more brightly coloured with russet or yellowish-brown. The rodents in this group are also known as narrow-footed thicket rats.

Similar There are at least 6 more species of woodland thicket rat in the region and these are very similar; 2 species of broad-footed thicket rat occur in limited areas of western Uganda and could cause confusion where ranges overlap. Acacia rat (*Thallomys paedulcus*) found in similar habitat but bigger than thicket rat.

Habitat Forest and dense woodland, but also more open woodland fringing on savanna that has tall grass and secondary scrub.

Behaviour Nocturnal and mainly arboreal. They construct nests of grass and other fine plant material in vegetation tangles up to 4 m above the ground but usually no more than 2 m. Also make use of tree holes and occasionally weaver-bird nests. A solitary rodent, except when a female has young. Average home range in a Ugandan study found to be 600–650 m².

Food Green plant material, flowers, fruits and seeds but also some insects.

Reproduction In Uganda pregnant females are recorded from May to July and November, but, at least in some areas, young may be dropped at any time of year. Litter size usually 2–4, rarely 7, pups weighing an average 4.2 g. Gestation averages 24 days.

Longevity In captivity >4 years.

Calls Typical mouse-like twittering and squeaks, normally not heard by humans.

Occurrence Common, widespread and occur in many parks and reserves.

MEASUREMENTS
Weight: 30-60 g
Total length: 21–33 cm
Tail length: 13–20 cm

EGYPTIAN SPINY MOUSE

Acomys cahirinus

Swahili: – German: *Ägyptische Stachelmaus* French: *Souris épineuse égyptienne*

Identification pointers Typical mouse-like appearance, but immediately recognisable by sharp, spiny hair growing on the back. Tail shorter than head and body and, as it breaks easily, a fairly high number in a population may have shortened tails. Ears are quite large, erect and rounded, and are often torn. Upperparts grey-brown to yellowish-grey, with off-white to white underparts.

Similar Perhaps as many as 7 different species of spiny mouse occur in East Africa, all easily identified, but most are difficult to separate from the Egyptian.

Habitat Semi-arid and desert areas, often in rocky habitats with sparse vegetation cover.

Behaviour Terrestrial; mainly nocturnal but with some diurnal activity. In small mixed colonies; densities quite high in suitable habitats. Rock crevices are important dens but also burrows dug by other small rodents, as well as termitaria.

Near shelters large accumulations of inedible food remains found, e.g. snail shells, millipede segments, seed husks. Tame readily; breed prolifically in captivity.

Food Opportunistic feeders that eat a variety of seeds, leaves, flowers, as well as a range of invertebrates, including insects, spiders, millipedes and small land snails.

Reproduction Probably breed throughout the year in the region and litters usually comprise 1–5 young, weighing about 7 g at birth after a relatively long gestation of some 35–42 days. Pups' eyes are open at birth, or at most 3 days later. Other females help a birthing female by cleaning newborns and also biting the umbilical.

Longevity Average 3 years, but up to 5.

Calls Squeaks, though seldom heard.

Occurrence One or more species widely found in East Africa and sometimes common. Egyptian found in Samburu, Meru, Marsabit (Kenya).

MEASUREMENTS
Weight: 11–33 g
Total length: 12–18 cm
Tail length: 5–8 cm

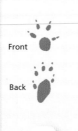

Front

Back

■ *Acomys cahirinus*
■ Other spiny mouse spp.

GREATER (MARSH) CANE-RAT

Thryonomys swinderianus

Swahili: *Ndezi, Nkungusi* **German:** *Große Rohrratte* **French:** *Grand aulacode*

Identification pointers Large, coarse-haired, stockily built rodents with short tails. Upperparts and sides usually dark speckled or grizzled-brown; underparts may be off-white to greyish-brown. Body hair falls out easily if handled. Fleshy, hair-covered pad on the snout extends beyond the nostrils; used in aggressive butting bouts between individuals.

Similar Lesser (savanna) cane-rat (*T. gregorianus*) about half size of greater cane-rat; utilises drier habitats, but the 2 species often live in close proximity.

Habitat Occurs in reed beds and other dense vegetation near water, especially within marshes and swamps.

Behaviour Mainly nocturnal although there is often some late afternoon and early morning activity where disturbance levels are low. Tend to forage alone, but live in loosely associated groups. In 1 study groups were shown to occupy territories of 3 000–4 000 m². Distinct runs are formed within feeding areas, radiating from the dense vegetation within which they usually den down. Characteristic droppings and small piles of reed segments from feeding are scattered throughout their home range. Surprisingly agile on land and can swim well.

Food Mostly roots, leaves, stems and shoots of grasses, reeds and sedges. Can be serious pest to sugar cane farmers.

Reproduction In East Africa it appears there are 2 breeding seasons tied to the rains (March to November). 1–8 young (average 4), 80–190 g, dropped after average 155 days. Young fully haired, with eyes open and are soon able to run about.

Longevity Just over 4 years in captivity.

Calls Distinctive whistle; also thump ground with hind feet.

Occurrence Occur in most parks and reserves within range. Despite being heavily hunted in some areas, they are generally common in suitable habitats.

MEASUREMENTS
Weight: 3–9 kg
Total length: 65–80 cm
Tail length: 15–20 cm

Front — 40 mm

Back — 80 mm

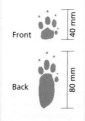

GAMBIAN GIANT RAT

Cricetomys gambianus

Swahili: *Buku* **German:** *Gambia-Riesenhamsterratte* **French:** *Rat de Gambie*

Identification pointers Large rat-like rodent with distinctive long whip-like tail that is white for slightly less than half of its length towards the tip. Upperparts grey to grey-brown, underparts lighter but not white. Hair around the eye forms dark ring and ears are large, thin and mobile.

Similar Forest giant rat (*C. emini*), present only in Uganda, has soft grey upperparts and white underparts. Exotic brown and black rats are smaller and have no white on the tail.

Habitat Forest and woodland on plains and on mountain slopes; also in urban areas, as well as rocky outcrops. On Mt Elgon reach altitudes of about 3 500 m; said to be common up to 2 100 m in the Ruwenzori.

Behaviour Nocturnal, but may be active during the early morning and late afternoon if undisturbed. Dig own burrows or use holes dug by other species; also live in tree holes or among root systems and plant debris. May accumulate substantial stores of food that they transport to their shelters in large cheek-pouches. Mainly terrestrial, but climb well. Often believed to be solitary, but several individuals may live in the same burrow system or shelter.

Food Fruit, roots, leaves and seeds (including cultivated crops) make up bulk of their diet; insects, snails and crabs also eaten.

Reproduction Non-seasonal; 1–5 young, about 20 g, born after 30–32 days.

Longevity A captive individual lived for 7 years and 10 months; other records mention 4 years.

Calls Generally silent though male makes a piping call.

Occurrence Common and widespread; found in many parks and reserves. Hunted in some areas for its tender meat.

MEASUREMENTS
Weight: 1–3 kg
Total length: 70–80 cm
Tail length: 36–46 cm

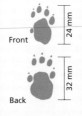

Front — 24 mm

Back — 32 mm

POUCHED MOUSE

Saccostomus campestris

Swahili: – **German:** *Kurzschwanz-Hamsterratte* **French:** *Saccostomus*

Identification pointers Round and fat-bodied, with soft, silky grey or greyish-brown fur. Underparts and lower face are white. Tail length much less than head-and-body length and legs are short. Ears are short and rounded and eyes small. Variable in size and colour throughout range. Has large expandable cheek pouches for transporting food to the burrow. In build and form bears strong resemblance to domesticated hamster.

Similar A second species *S. mearnsi* also occurs widely in East Africa; differs only in having grey not white underparts.

Habitat Wide habitat tolerance but prefer soft, particularly sandy, soils. Found in open or dense vegetation, as well as rocky areas. Distribution seems linked to the need for soft, easily excavated soils.

Behaviour Generally solitary, although they may live in loose colonies. Dig their own burrows but will also use burrows excavated by other species, also seeking shelter in termite mounds, logs and rock piles. Use food pouches in cheeks (shopping baskets) to take substantial quantities of food to shelter or burrow where it can be eaten in relative safety from predators, or stored for future use. Quite slow moving and amazingly easy to catch by hand; but otherwise quite difficult to trap. Nocturnal and terrestrial.

Food Mainly seeds, small wild fruits and occasionally insects.

Reproduction After gestation of about 20 days, 2–10 fully haired young, each less than 3 g, are born. Litters probably dropped at any time of year in the region.

Longevity <3 years usual.

Calls Normally silent, but typical mouse-like chittering and squeaks if handled.

Occurrence Widespread in the region, but, because it is quite difficult to trap, is poorly represented in museum collections. Probably fairly common and present in many protected areas.

MEASUREMENTS
Weight: 45 g (to 85 g)
Total length: 15–26 cm
Tail length: 5 cm

131

SOFT-FURRED RATS

Mastomys and *Praomys* spp.

Swahili: – **German:** *Vielzitzenmäuse* **French:** *Praomys*

Identification pointers A complex of at least 8 species of very similar mice (also sometimes called multimammate mice) that may often be one of the dominant species in any given area. In many cases they can only be separated by chromosome analysis. All are typically mouse-like, rather nondescript and without any distinctive features. The hair is usually soft and dense, ranging in colour from blackish-grey, greyish, various shades of brown, reddish-brown to yellowish.

Similar Could be confused with a number of other groups and even experts have identification problems with this group. In most cases it is not possible to identify them to species level in the field.

Habitat Some species have a very wide habitat tolerance, while others are more specialised in their requirements.

Behaviour Most are nocturnal and terrestrial, with some species such as the Natal multimammate mouse (*Mastomys natalensis*) often associated with human activities and structures. Many excavate their own burrow systems and may form substantial colonies. In periods of plenty they may irrupt, reaching plague proportions. Certain species are considered to be important carriers of diseases that impact on humans.

Reproduction Some species may breed year-round; others may be more seasonal. A species occurring in southern Africa, *M. coucha,* is one of the most fecund mammals on earth with up to 22 foetuses in a single female, although 6–12 is more usual for the group. Average gestation within the group is 20–24 days.

Longevity >5 years for a West African species in captivity; this is probably a maximum age for the group.

Calls Mouse-like squeaks.

Occurrence A number of species common to abundant, a few with restricted habitats.

MEASUREMENTS
Weight: 20–60 g
Total length: 20–25 cm
Tail length: 10–14 cm

BUSHVELD GERBIL

Tatera leucogaster

Swahili: – **German:** *Rennmaus* **French:** *Gerbille du bushveld*

Identification pointers Fairly large, with tail about half of total length, well-developed hind legs and feet, the soles of latter being naked – hence alternative name of naked-soled gerbil. Ears longer than broad, and eyes fairly large. Tail usually has dark dorsal line and is darkish-haired towards tip. Upperparts usually reddish-brown to yellow-brown, with off-white to white underparts. Bushveld gerbil only found in south-west Tanzania.

Similar In region 6 other naked-footed gerbil species occur, all similar but differing in colour of hair at tail-tip, with Boehm's having a white tassel. Narrow ears help identify this species and group.

Habitat Strong preference for areas with sandy soils in a wide range of habitats. Within its range is associated mainly with mixed open woodland and grassland.

Behaviour Nocturnal and terrestrial, digging extensive burrow systems and living in loosely knit colonies. They dig 2 types of burrow – shallow bolt holes and deeper living quarters. Main burrows terminate in a chamber that may be lined with grass. Surface runways are usually distinctive and may extend some distance to feeding areas. When food is abundant, populations may reach very high levels. Considered important vectors of bubonic plague in parts of their total range.

Food Grass seed important; digs out small bulbs and roots; also eats green plant material. Probably eats some insects.

Reproduction After gestation of about 22–25 days, 2–9 young is usual litter size, with an average of 4–5. Breeding season probably tied to onset of rains.

Longevity Not known, but an Asian species in captivity has lived for 7 years.

Calls None recorded.

Occurrence Serengeti, Ngorongoro, Katavi, Ruaha (Tanzania). Abundant, but populations fluctuate; eaten in some areas.

MEASUREMENTS
Weight: 70 g
Total length: 25–30 cm
Tail length: 13–17 cm

FAT MOUSE

Steatomys pratensis

Swahili: – **German:** *Fettmaus* **French:** *Steatomys*

Identification pointers Quite small, dumpy mice with tail about a third of total length. Upperparts usually rusty-brown to sandy-brown and underparts white, as are upper surfaces of feet. Fur along back often a somewhat darker shade. Tail usually darker above than below. Take their name from ability to lay down thick fat deposits under skin and around organs, at which time they appear almost round.

Similar At least 1 other *Steatomys* species, the so-called 'tiny fat mouse', occurs in the region but is near impossible to separate in the field. Pouched mouse much bigger and with grey upperparts.

Habitat Wide range of habitats; but favours areas with sandy soils; commonly associated with cultivated fields.

Behaviour Nocturnal and terrestrial, apparently living singly or in pairs. Dig their own burrows, but do not form true colonies. Well adapted to drought as not only can they build up fat deposits, but they are also able to reduce their body temperature to lower metabolism and live on fat reserves. Unlike the pouched mouse, fat mice do not have cheek-pouches in which to carry food, but they do carry surplus to their burrows.

Food Primarily seeds, but small bulbs and roots dug up too; also some green plant material and insects.

Reproduction Probably tied to the rainy season, but little known in the region. Litters of 1–9 young recorded; 3–4 more usual, weighing about 1.5 g at birth.

Longevity An individual lived 3 years in captivity.

Calls Typical mouse-like squeaks, seldom heard by humans.

Occurrence Widespread and often common, but quite heavily hunted as a food delicacy, especially when fat deposits at best. In virtually all parks and reserves in range.

MEASUREMENTS
Weight: 26 g
Total length: 8–15 cm
Tail length: 3–6 cm

NILE GRASS (KUSU) RAT

Arvicanthis niloticus

Swahili: – **German:** *Nil-Grasratte* **French:** *Rat roussard du Nil*

Identification pointers Fair-sized rats with coarse coats. May be black-chestnut, grey-olive or have paler upperparts and greyish underparts. In some parts of region underparts paler to white, but this seems to be a rarity. Overall appearance is of a grizzled coat, pencilled with black. Fairly large, blunt head; rounded and red-brown backed ears and smallish eyes.

Similar Several similar species of Nile grass rat exist in East Africa and are difficult to separate; African vlei- or swamp-rats (*Otomys* spp.), of which there are 6 species in the region, often share same habitat; have larger, blunter heads, shorter tails and usually darker coat.

Habitat Strongly associated with different types of grassland, chiefly within savanna; usually at lower altitudes, also in some highlands. Prefer dense ground cover but will occupy rocky locations.

Behaviour Will dig their own burrows; also shelter in rock crevices, termitaria and fallen logs. Pathways radiate out from shelters to feeding grounds. Nests of grass are built in these shelters, or on surface among dense vegetation. Nocturnal and diurnal, but most activity seems to take place at night. Loose colonies; number of animals seems to be restricted in any given burrow system. In optimum conditions, populations may explode to hundreds of individuals per hectare.

Food Seeds, leaves and grasses make up the bulk of their diet and small piles of cut grass indicate their presence.

Reproduction During the rains (possibly year-round in some areas), females probably drop several litters of 4–6 pups, rarely more. Gestation 18–22 days; birth weight of young is 3–6 g.

Longevity A captive individual lived for 6 years and 8 months.

Calls None recorded.

Occurrence Common in most parks and reserves within its range.

MEASUREMENTS
Weight: 50–120 g
Total length: 20–35 cm
Tail: 10–15 cm

CAPE HARE
SAVANNA HARE

Lepus capensis
Lepus victoriae

Swahili: *Sungura* **German:** *Kaphase, Savannenhase* **French:** *Lièvre*

Identification pointers In East Africa both species similar in size and appearance and difficult, if not impossible, to separate in the field. Best identified by their different habitat preferences. Both have typical hare-like appearance: long, well-developed hind legs, long ears and a short tail that is white below and black above. Body colour is brown-grey, flecked white but variable. Underparts are white; they usually have a reddish-brown patch on the back of the neck.

Similar Bunyoro rabbit (*Poelagus marjorita*) in Uganda has shorter hind legs and ears; Smith's red rock rabbit (*Pronolagus rupestris*) has shorter ears and hind legs, and uniform reddish-brown tail, found in hilly country of central Tanzania and marginally in south-west Kenya.

Habitat Cape hare has strong preference for open areas, especially shorter grassland; savanna hare favours woodland and bush cover with grass.

Behaviour Mainly nocturnal and crepuscular, but may be active on overcast days. By day they lie up in forms (shallow indentations in the ground made by the body). In ideal habitats may occur in large numbers, although they are solitary animals. Rely on their camouflage when approached, running away at the last minute and usually zig-zagging at speed.

Food Mainly grasses; also other plants.

Reproduction Usually several litters; 1–3 leverets dropped at any time of year, after about 42-days; the well-developed young can move around soon after birth.

Longevity 10–12 years, although usually less in the wild.

Calls Normally silent, but if injured or caught they scream.

Occurrence Both hare species very common and occur in most East African wildlife reserves.

MEASUREMENTS
Weight: 1.4–3.5 kg
Total length: 45–60 cm
Tail: 7–14 cm

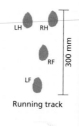

LH RH

RF

LF

300 mm

Running track

■ Cape hare only
■ Savanna hare only
■ Distribution overlap

SMITH'S RED ROCK RABBIT

Pronolagus rupestris

Swahili: – **German:** *Smith-Rotkaninchen* **French:** *Lièvre roux de Smith*

Identification pointers Typical rabbit-like appearance, with long ears (shorter than those of hares), hind legs longer than the front legs and soft, dense fur. Grizzled grey-brown upperparts and reddish-brown on flanks, limbs and tail, with lighter underparts. Ears grey to grey-brown; on nape between ears there is usually a patch of reddish fur.

Similar Generally separated from hare species by habitat; hares have longer ears and black and white tails. Rock hyraxes share habitat but have very short rounded ears and no visible tail.

Habitat Restricted to rocky areas on hillslopes and mountainsides, including isolated rock outcrops with good grass and scrub cover.

Behaviour Mainly nocturnal, but they will sunbask and forage when it's overcast. During the day they lie up in a form created by weight of body, or in rock crevices and among boulder clusters. Solitary foragers, but in suitable habitat several animals may live in close proximity. They deposit lozenge-shaped droppings in middens that may cover several square metres.

Food Mainly grass, but leaves of shrubs when little else available.

Reproduction Nothing known in region but possibly not seasonal. Young (1–2) are near naked and helpless at birth and are dropped in a cup-shaped nest lined with the belly fur of the female.

Longevity Not known.

Calls Said to give loud screams when alarmed.

Occurrence Probably secure and quite common in some areas. Ngorongoro, Ruaha (Tanzania); Hell's Gate (Kenya).

MEASUREMENTS
Weight: 1.3–2 kg
Total length: 43–65 cm
Tail length: 5–11 cm

LH RH

RF

LF

Running track

INDO-PACIFIC HUMPBACK DOLPHIN

Sousa chinensis

Swahili: – **German:** *Buckeldelfin* **French:** *Dauphin à bosse du Pacifique*

Identification pointers Easily distinguished from other long-beaked dolphins by long thickened ridge, or hump, along middle of back, supporting a small, pointed dorsal fin. In region most animals are coloured dark-grey to brown-black with underparts off-white to grey and sometimes with pinkish tinge. Slow swimmers and will spy-hop. Snout usually first part of animal to break surface.

Similar Other dolphins in the region lack the hump on the back.

Habitat Usually inshore in water shallower than 25 m; sheltered bays, estuaries, sandbanks, mangrove swamps.

Behaviour In groups of 1–30, but usually 3–7 individuals, with much movement in and out of groups. Forage close inshore, favouring shallow water. Rarely seem to venture more than a few hundred metres from shore. Dives usually last for < 1 minute, but up to 5 minutes on record. Virtually nothing known in East Africa, but there may be some seasonal movements along the coastline between suitable locations, as is known in some other areas.

Food Small fish, squid, octopus and crustaceans.

Reproduction Cows give birth to calves at any time of year but with a possible summer peak in the region. A single calf is dropped after 10–12-month gestation and they are usually weaned at the age of 2 years. Birth length is about 1 m and weight around 14 kg.

Longevity >40 years recorded.

Calls Few audible on surface except for popping and belching sounds.

Conservation Quite vulnerable to disturbances, such as boats, and probably illegally hunted in the region. Not uncommonly sighted in sheltered bays and areas with mangroves.

MEASUREMENTS
Weight: 280 kg
Total length: 1.8 –3 m

138

INDIAN OCEAN BOTTLENOSED DOLPHIN *Tursiops aduncus*

Swahili: – **German:** *Großer Tümmler* **French:** *Grand dauphin*

Identification pointers A large, robust dolphin with a tall, curved dorsal fin and a medium-length beak that is wide and rounded at the tip. Lower jaw projects slightly beyond upper jaw. Upperparts usually uniform dark grey, with paler grey sides and underparts. There is usually a thin, pale line running from eye to flipper, but often indistinct.

Similar There are 2 very similar bottle-nosed dolphin species (*T. aduncus* and *T. tursiops*) that have inshore and off-shore populations, but *T. aduncus* is the most likely one to be seen along the East African coastline. Inshore populations of both species difficult to separate on sighting alone. Should be easy to separate from humpback dolphin and more brightly marked long-beaked common dolphin. Common dolphin character-ised by hourglass-shaped pattern on sides, and frequent breaching. In small groups or pods of several thousand.

Habitat Mainly in coastal waters <20 m deep, but also enters estuaries and mangroves.

Behaviour Typical pod size 5–15 (some give 20–50) animals, but sometimes hundreds and up to 1 000 may gather. Commonly mix with other dolphin species. Have been observed in co-operative hunting where a pod drives shoals of fish to the shore or onto a sandbank.

Food Mostly fish and squid, taken mainly from the sea floor.

Reproduction Single calf (about 1 m long, weighing 14 kg) born after about 1-years' gestation. Seasonality not known in region, but births could possibly occur throughout the year.

Longevity 43 years recorded.

Calls Very vocal animals, but rarely heard on surface.

Conservation Common, but local hunt-ing and accidental bycatch may have some influence on local populations.

MEASUREMENTS
Weight: 230 kg
 (inshore Indo-Pacific)
Total length: 2.5–2.6 m

DUGONG

Dugong dugon

Swahili: *Nguva* **German:** *Dugong* **French:** *Dugong*

Identification pointers A large, cigar-shaped aquatic mammal that never comes onto land. Forelimbs are paddle-like flippers and hindlimbs are absent. It has a large, fleshy, boneless tail, flattened horizontally. Skin greyish-brown with a few sparsely scattered bristles. Upperparts slightly darker than underparts. Large disc-like front of mouth and lower lip is covered with short, thick bristles.

Similar Should not be confused with any species in the region, as seals are absent and all dolphins in area are sleeker, with pointed snouts and a dorsal fin.

Habitat Shallow, sheltered waters close to the coastline with extensive seagrass beds.

Behaviour Usually seen singly, in pairs or in family parties, but groups of up to 30 animals sometimes seen. They are slow swimmers, cruising at about 2 knots, but can put on bursts of speed (5 knots) to escape danger. Can remain submerged for up to 5 minutes, but 1 minute is usual when feeding. Said to prefer to feed in the shallows on a rising tide.

Food Consume several species of seagrass in sheltered shallow bays and lagoons. Eat up to 15% of their body weight each day. Some animal food has been found in the stomachs of dead dugongs, but this may be accidental intake.

Reproduction Single young (very rarely twins) dropped after 11–13-month gestation. Young weigh up to 35 kg; mother suckles offspring for up to 18 months. Little recorded on seasonality, but some reports indicate births November to January.

Longevity Up to 73 years in the wild.

Calls Fairly vocal but rarely heard.

Conservation Numbers greatly reduced in region by direct hunting and accidental deaths in fishing nets. Found in estuaries and mouths of major rivers such as the Rufiji in Tanzania, Lamu/Malindi area, and Pemba/Unguja channel (Zanzibar Archipelago).

MEASUREMENTS
Weight: 350–500 kg
Total length: 2.5–3 m

DUNG IDENTIFICATION

Droppings, and sometimes the way they are deposited, may help in identifying a mammal that is no longer in sight. Included here is a selection of those droppings that you are most likely to encounter.

Note that the match used for comparison in some photographs is 43 mm in length. Unless stated otherwise, measurements apply to length of dung. Measurements given are averages.

ELEPHANT: Variable size. Barrel-shaped. Often >200 mm. Deposited at random.

SQUARE-LIPPED RHINO: 150 mm. Barrel-shaped. Bulls deposit dung in middens, often along roadsides.

 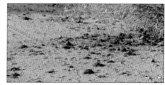

HOOK-LIPPED RHINO: 100 mm. Barrel-shaped. The middens often show clear scuffing left by hind feet.

HIPPOPOTAMUS: 100 mm. Barrel-shaped. Scattered across range. Males flick dung onto bushes/grass with tail.

GREVY'S ZEBRA: 55 mm. Kidney-shaped. Scattered heaps. Stallions deposit faeces in middens.

PLAINS ZEBRA: 50 mm. Kidney-shaped. Deposited in scattered heaps.

WARTHOG: 50 mm. Kidney-shaped. Scattered in small heaps.

BUSHPIG: Up to 80 mm. Variable. Usually scatters oblong pellets.

GIANT FOREST HOG: Variable size. Scattered and in communal middens; very similar to bushpig.

BUFFALO: Variable size and similar to domestic cattle (cow pats). Scattered.

DROMEDARY: 27 mm. Rounded and left in scattered heaps.

GIRAFFE: 30 mm. Heaps usually more scattered than those of eland or greater kudu.

GREATER KUDU: 20 mm. Leaves scattered heaps. Concentrated in shade.

BLUE WILDEBEEST: 20 mm. Scattered heaps. Territorial bulls leave large accumulations.

COMMON ELAND: 25 mm. Scattered heaps. No middens.

LICHTENSTEIN'S HARTEBEEST: 18 mm. Scattered heaps. Bulls form middens.

COKE'S HARTEBEEST: 18 mm. Scattered heaps. Bulls form middens.

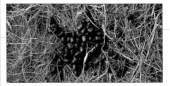

BONGO: 22 mm. Scattered heaps.

BEISA ORYX: 18 mm. Scattered heaps and male middens.

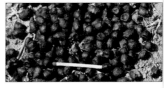

IMPALA: 12–14 mm. Scattered heaps and breeding ram middens.

PUKU: 16 mm. Scattered heaps. Pellets often clumped.

BUSHBUCK: 14 mm. Scattered heaps.

KLIPSPRINGER: 10 mm. Always in communal middens.

KLIPSPRINGER: Communal midden.

MOUNTAIN REEDBUCK: 12–14 mm. Scattered heaps.

THOMSON'S GAZELLE: 12 mm. Scattered heaps.

ORIBI: 12 mm. Scattered and in middens.

RED DUIKER : 9 mm. Several heaps close together.

BLUE DUIKER: 7 mm. Forms loose middens, but separate heaps.

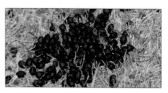

COMMON DUIKER: 11 mm. Concentrated heaps in loose middens.

STEENBOK: 7–10 mm. Only antelope that fully buries droppings.

KIRK'S DIK-DIK: 7 mm. Family groups use communal middens.

SAVANNA BABOON: Variable size. Scattered, but accumulations at roosts.

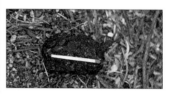

VERVET MONKEY: Variable size. Scattered.

PORCUPINE: 40–70 mm long. Dropped in clusters of joined pellets, at random.

CAPE CLAWLESS OTTER: 22–30 mm in diameter. Lighten with age; middens close to water.

LION: 40 mm in diameter. Scattered.

LEOPARD: 20–35 mm in diameter. Scattered and in loose middens.

CHEETAH: 25–35 mm in diameter. Scattered and in loose middens.

SPOTTED HYAENA: 30–40 mm in diameter. Scattered and in loose middens. Whiten with age.

AARDWOLF: 35 mm in diameter. Concentrated middens.

BAT-EARED FOX: 18 mm in diameter. Often in concentrated middens at dens.

BLACK-BACKED JACKAL: 20 mm in diameter. Scattered.

WHITE-TAILED MONGOOSE: 18 mm in diameter. Scattered and loose middens.

DWARF MONGOOSE: 8 mm in diameter. In middens close to dens.

SMALL-SPOTTED GENET: 15 mm in diameter. Usually in compact middens.

AFRICAN CIVET: Variable size. Always in middens – 'civetries'.

STRIPED POLECAT: Usually <12 mm in diameter and often 'twisted'. Scattered.

WHITE-BELLIED HEDGEHOG: <10 mm in diameter. Scattered.

CAPE HARE: 10 mm in diameter. Lozenge-shaped; scattered heaps.

SMITH'S RED ROCK RABBIT: 10–15 mm in diameter. Lozenge-shaped; large middens.

ROCK HYRAX: 10 mm in diameter. Dropped in large middens close to shelter.

YELLOW-SPOTTED ROCK HYRAX: 10 mm in diameter. Always in large middens.

HYRAX: Urine streaks very characteristic. Always found near dung middens.

AARDVARK: Variable size and shape. Often buried.

EAST AFRICAN SPRINGHARE: 15–20 mm. Somewhat flattened. Small, scattered heaps.

GREATER (MARSH) CANE-RAT: 20 mm in length. Scattered heaps. Groove on one pellet surface.

EGYPTIAN FREE-TAILED BAT: 8 mm in length. Scattered and concentrated at roosts.

TRACK COMPARISONS

HANDS & FEET

SENEGAL GALAGO (BUSHBABY)

30 mm

Right hind

DWARF GALAGO

20 mm

Right hind

THICK-TAILED GALAGO

50 mm

Back

SAVANNA BABOON

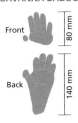

Front

80 mm

Back

140 mm

VERVET MONKEY

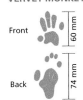

Front

60 mm

Back

74 mm

SYKES'S MONKEY

Front

65 mm

Back

80 mm

COLOBUS

Front

Back

140 mm

CHIMPANZEE

190 mm

Back

GORILLA

Front

Back

275 mm

HYRAX

Front

30 mm

Back

50 mm

CAPE CLAWLESS OTTER

Front

106 mm

Back

108 mm

LARGE HERBIVORES

GREVY'S ZEBRA

Front

100 mm

PLAINS ZEBRA

Front

90 mm

HOOK-LIPPED RHINOCEROS

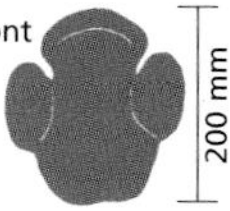

Front

200 mm

SQUARE-LIPPED RHINOCEROS

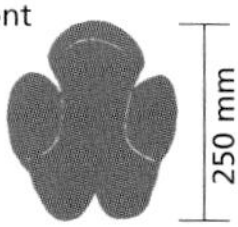

Front

250 mm

COMMON HIPPOPOTAMUS

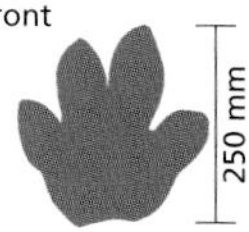

Front

250 mm

SAVANNA ELEPHANT

Front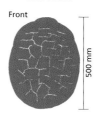

500 mm

DROMEDARY

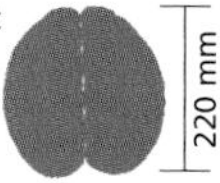

Front

220 mm

EVEN-TOED HOOVED ANIMALS

COMMON WARTHOG

Front

45 mm

BUSHPIG

Front

55 mm

RED RIVER HOG

Front

55 mm

GIANT FOREST HOG

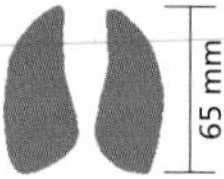

Front

65 mm

GIRAFFE

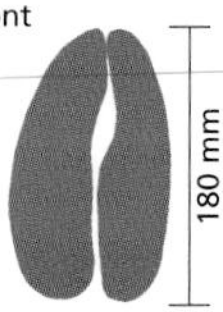

Front

180 mm

AFRICAN BUFFALO

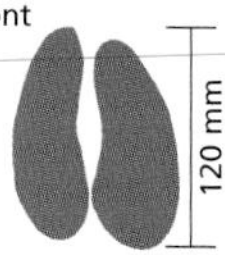

Front

120 mm

COMMON ELAND

Front

100 mm

BONGO

Front

80 mm

GREATER KUDU

Front

68 mm

LESSER KUDU

Front

52 mm

SITATUNGA

Front

120-180 mm

BEISA ORYX

Front

110 mm

ROAN ANTELOPE

Front

120 mm

SABLE ANTELOPE

Front

115 mm

WATERBUCK

Front

90 mm

COKE'S HARTEBEEST

Front

100 mm

LICHTENSTEIN'S HARTEBEEST

Front

100 mm

TOPI

Front

90 mm

BLUE WILDEBEEST

Front

100 mm

KOB

Front

67 mm

PUKU

Front

67 mm

BUSHBUCK

Front

44 mm

BOHOR REEDBUCK

Front

45 mm

COMMON REEDBUCK

Front

65 mm

MOUNTAIN REEDBUCK
Front
43 mm

IMPALA
Front
47 mm

GERENUK
Front
45 mm

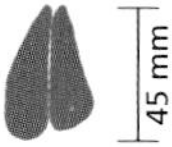

SOEMMERING'S GAZELLE
Front
56 mm

GRANT'S GAZELLE
Front
51 mm

THOMSON'S GAZELLE
Front
48 mm

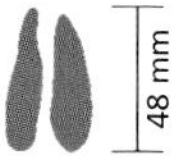

ORIBI
Front
40 mm

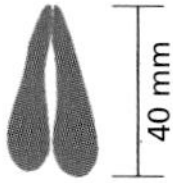

STEENBOK
Front
40 mm

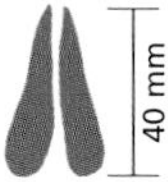

SUNI
Front
23 mm

SHARPE'S GRYSBOK
Front
34 mm

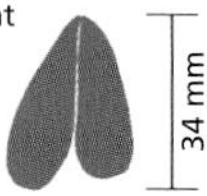

KLIPSPRINGER
Front
20 mm

KIRK'S DIK-DIK
Front
21 mm

GUENTHER'S DIK-DIK
Front
21 mm

COMMON DUIKER
Front
38 mm

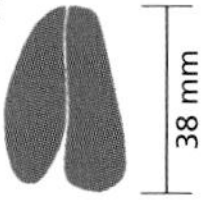

ADER'S DUIKER
Front
30 mm

RED DUIKER
Front
30 mm

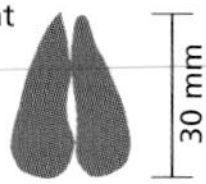

BLUE DUIKER
Front
24 mm

THREE TOES VISIBLE

AARDVARK

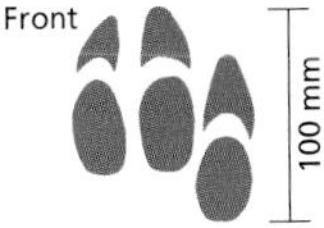

Front

100 mm

SPRINGHARE

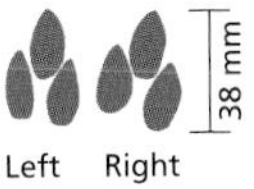

38 mm

Left   Right

PAWS WITH CLAWS

BAT-EARED FOX

Front

39 mm

BLACK-BACKED JACKAL

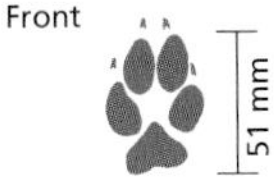

Front

51 mm

SIDE-STRIPED JACKAL

Front

43 mm

GOLDEN JACKAL

Front

43 mm

WILD DOG

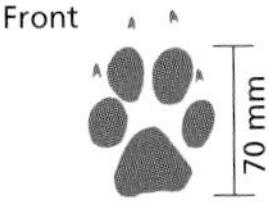

Front

70 mm

CHEETAH

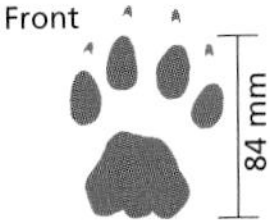

Front

84 mm

SPOTTED-NECKED OTTER

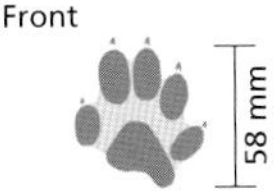

Front

58 mm

HONEY BADGER

Front

54 mm

PORCUPINE

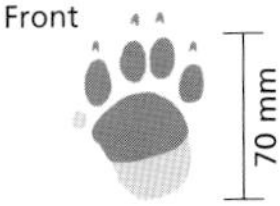

Front

70 mm

AFRICAN CIVET

Front

45 mm

STRIPED POLECAT

Front

22 mm

SLENDER MONGOOSE

Front

23 mm

WHITE-TAILED MONGOOSE

Front

41 mm

WATER MONGOOSE

Front

41 mm

SMITH'S RED ROCK RABBIT

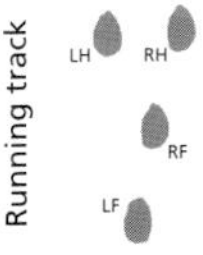

Running track

LH   RH

RF

LF

CAPE HARE

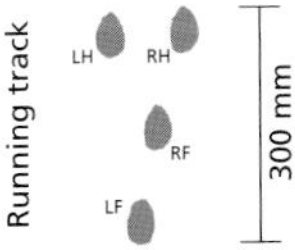

Running track

LH   RH

RF

LF

300 mm

151

WESTERN GROUND SQUIRREL

Front

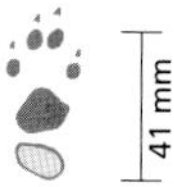

41 mm

TREE SQUIRREL

Front

25 mm

GREATER CANE-RAT

Front

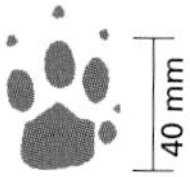

40 mm

GAMBIAN GIANT RAT

Front

24 mm

FOUR-TOED SENGI

Front

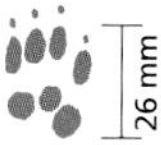

26 mm

GOLDEN-RUMPED SENGI

Front

32 mm

SHORT-SNOUTED SENGI

Front

7 mm

SPECTACLED SENGI

Front

7 mm

WHITE-BELLIED HEDGEHOG

Front

18 mm

WHITE-TOOTHED SHREW

Front

MOUSE

Front

10 mm

PAWS – NO CLAWS

COMMON LARGE-SPOTTED GENET

Front

22 mm

SMALL-SPOTTED GENET

Front

22 mm

CARACAL

Front

47 mm

SERVAL

Front

47 mm

LION

Front

128 mm

LEOPARD

Front

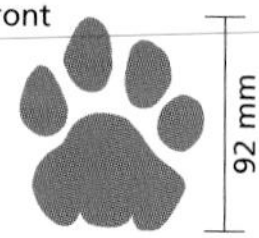

92 mm

GLOSSARY

Aquatic Living mainly, or entirely, in water.

Arboreal Living in trees.

Browser An animal that eats shoots and leaves of trees, bushes and shrubs.

Carnivore Meat-eating animal.

Crepuscular Active in twilight.

Diurnal Active during daylight hours.

Erectile Capable of being raised to an erect position.

Foraging Searching for food.

Gestation Period of development of young within the uterus; conception to birth.

Grazer An animal that eats grasses.

Grizzled Sprinkled, or streaked, with grey or white hairs.

Home range Area in which an animal normally lives and carries out its day-to-day activities.

Midden Place where droppings/scats are regularly deposited.

Nocturnal Active during the hours of darkness.

Oestrus Period during which female mammal is sexually receptive to males.

Omnivore Animal with a varied diet that includes both animals and plants.

Rut Period of sexual excitement in male animals; associated with mating season.

Sounder Collective name given to pigs.

Species Group of interbreeding individuals of common ancestry, reproductively isolated from other groups.

Terrestrial Living on land.

Territory Area defended from intruders by an individual or group.

SUGGESTED FURTHER READING

Bryant, L. 1989. *Rowland Ward's African Records of Big Game* (21 ed.). Rowland Ward, San Antonio, Texas.

Kingdon, J. 1971–1982. *East African Mammals: An Atlas of Evolution in Africa* (Volumes 1–3). Academic Press, London.

Stuart, Chris & Tilde. 2001. *A Field Guide to the Tracks and Signs of Southern and East African Wildlife*. Struik, Cape Town.

Stuart, Chris & Tilde. 2006. *Field Guide to the Larger Mammals of Africa*. Struik, Cape Town.

INDEX

SCIENTIFIC NAMES

SWAHILI COMMON NAMES

GERMAN COMMON NAMES

FRENCH COMMON NAMES

PHOTOGRAPHIC CREDITS

Alan Weaving: page 67; Ardea London Ltd/Alan Weaving: page 20 (left); Ariadne van Zandbergen/IOA: page 56; Jabruson/Naturepl.com: page 22 (right); Daryl & Sharna Balfour/IOA: Front cover; Duncan Butchart: page 13 (inset); FLPA / Terry Whittaker: page 25; Galen Rathbun: pages 108, 109, 111; Gallo Images: page 20 (right); Gallo/Lorna Stanton: pages 8 (right), 11 (right); Gallo/Richard du Toit, p 90; Harald Nicolay: page 87 (left) Harry van Rompaey: page 12, 17 (inset), 22 (left), 27; Ian Gaigher: page 86 (right); John Carlyon: page 116, 120; Klaus Rudloff: page 80, 121, 122; Mark Cawardine/Images of Africa: 139; Nature Picture Library/Photo Access: page 123 (left); Nigel Dennis/ IOA: back cover, third from top, page 34, 93; P.K. Anderson: 140; Pat Frere: page 24 (inset); Paul Vercammen: page 102; Peter Blackwell/IOA: page 23; Peter Jackson: page 21; Roland van Boxstaele: page 36; Roland Wirth: page 70; Shanan Atkins: page 138; Viv Wilson: page 26 (left); Walter Poduschka: page 112